EXAMPLES & EXPLANATIONS

Legal Research

Legal Research

Terrill Pollman

Professor of Law
William S. Boyd School of Law
University of Nevada, Las Vegas

Jeanne Frazier Price

Associate Dean of Academic Affairs
Professor of Law
Director of the Wiener-Rogers Law Library
William S. Boyd School of Law
University of Nevada, Las Vegas

Linda L. Berger

Associate Dean for Faculty Development and Research
Family Foundation Professor of Law
William S. Boyd School of Law
University of Nevada, Las Vegas

. Wolters Kluwer

Published by Wolters Kluwer in New York.

Wolters Kluwer Legal & Regulatory US serves customers worldwide with CCH, Aspen Publishers, and Kluwer Law International products. (www.WKLegaledu.com)

To contact Customer Service, e-mail customer.service@wolterskluwer.com, call 1-800-234-1660, fax 1-800-901-9075, or mail correspondence to:

> Wolters Kluwer
> Attn: Order Department
> PO Box 990
> Frederick, MD 21705

Printed in the United States of America.

1 2 3 4 5 6 7 8 9 0

ISBN 978-1-4548-6789-0

Library of Congress Cataloging-in-Publication Data

Names: Pollman, Terrill, 1948- author. | Price, Jeanne Frazier, author. | Berger, Linda L., author.
Title: Legal research / Terrill Pollman, Professor of Law William S. Boyd School of Law University of Nevada, Las Vegas; Jeanne Frazier Price, Associate Dean of Academic Affairs, William S. Boyd School of Law, University of Nevada, Las Vegas; Linda L. Berger, Associate Dean for Faculty Development and Research Family Foundation Professor of Law, William S. Boyd School of Law, University of Nevada, Las Vegas.
Description: New York : Wolters Kluwer, [2017] | Includes bibliographical references and index.
Identifiers: LCCN 2016043749 | ISBN 9781454867890 (alk. paper)
Subjects: LCSH: Legal research — United States.
Classification: LCC KF240.P65 2017 | DDC 340.072/073 — dc23
LC record available at https://lccn.loc.gov/2016043749

About Wolters Kluwer Legal & Regulatory US

Wolters Kluwer Legal & Regulatory US delivers expert content and solutions in the areas of law, corporate compliance, health compliance, reimbursement, and legal education. Its practical solutions help customers successfully navigate the demands of a changing environment to drive their daily activities, enhance decision quality, and inspire confident outcomes.

Serving customers worldwide, its legal and regulatory portfolio includes products under the Aspen Publishers, CCH Incorporated, Kluwer Law International, ftwilliam.com, and MediRegs names. They are regarded as exceptional and trusted resources for general legal and practice-specific knowledge, compliance and risk management, dynamic workflow solutions, and expert commentary.

To Ty, both of them
TP

To Alex, Giles, and Lorene
JFP

To Marjorie Rombauer
LLB

Summary of Contents

Contents

Acknowledgments

Linda Berger, Terry Pollman, and Jeanne Price thank the William S. Boyd School of Law and its Dean, Daniel W. Hamilton, for generous research support. We are grateful to our colleagues for thoughtful conversation and creative ideas on the law and the place of legal research in the life of a lawyer, and to our students for continually providing new insights to our own understanding of what we teach. We also thank Mary A. Lundeberg for giving us permission to use her wonderful research on reading.

We are fortunate to come from a rich community of librarians, professors, and scholars who focus on legal research and writing. So many in this community generously share expertise on both teaching and scholarship. We remain in their debt. We all agree that it is impossible to name the many individuals who have contributed to our vision of the complex relationships and connections in studying and writing about sources of law.

CHAPTER 1

Introduction

If we knew what it was we were doing, it would not be called research, would it?

— Albert Einstein

When one tugs at a single thing in nature, he finds it attached to the rest of the world.

— John Muir

Creativity is just connecting things. When you ask creative people how they did something, they feel a little guilty because they didn't really do it, they just saw something. It seemed obvious to them after a while. That's because they were able to connect experiences they've had and synthesize new things.

— Steve Jobs

Legal research is complex, and the myriad choices available online can overwhelm beginners with information. Although finding sources is not likely to be difficult in these days of ubiquitous internet use, understanding what you find is sometimes a challenge. We've structured the book around a few important ideas about research.

First, principles of weight of authority underlie all of the choices you make as you research. Understanding that sources have more or less persuasive power depending on where they come from and what your purpose is in using them is one important key to understanding how to choose sources wisely.

Next, legal sources do not exist in a vacuum. They exist both in relation to a specific context of rules and facts, and also in relation to other sources. Taking the weight, the connections, and the context into account is at the heart of successful research.

And finally, to understand a source, you need more than a definition of what that source is; you need to understand how lawyers use it and how they use the source in different contexts. Recognizing how lawyers use different sources as they analyze and write will inform the way you research.

OVERVIEW OF ORGANIZATION

If you are using this book as a text for a class, of course you'll follow the order for reading chapters that your professor sets out in the syllabus. If you're using the book as a study aid, however, let us explain the chronology we've chosen. Overall, we've structured the book to reflect weight of authority and the other ideas described above. As a general rule, we discuss sources in the order most attorneys would follow to research and write about legal questions. We start with principles of weight of authority because those principles apply to every source and every decision you make while researching. Then, although many novices and some attorneys might start with secondary sources to educate themselves a bit, students and attorneys with more expertise in an area would quickly turn to primary sources. There are two chapters on each of the most important types of primary authority: legislation, judicial opinions, and administrative regulations. The first chapter of the two will explain the basics; the second chapter will provide examples to illustrate research principles in action.

Next, the book addresses the ethical obligations involved in legal research, including your responsibility to accurately represent the state of the law, update sources, and follow a jurisdiction's rules. The book then turns to secondary sources. Finally, we suggest how to continue to learn and become a more expert researcher.

Two appendices offer further help. First, if you are having trouble finding sources, Appendix A has basic principles and tips on how to search for sources. These tips should help you gain confidence that you are finding what you need. Appendix B offers a very basic look at citation practices. Legal citation may look like gibberish to the uninitiated, but if a reader is quickly able — through citation practices — to identify the nature of a cited source, she is in a better position to understand how it fits into a legal argument and to assess the strength of the authority. Knowing the source to which a citation refers is essential to making good choices using the principles of weight of authority. Although far from comprehensive, Appendix B will help you decipher citations and begin to employ citation basics yourself.

ORGANIZATION WITHIN CHAPTERS

All of the chapters that introduce a source follow a pattern. Each begins with an introduction and then moves to a glossary. Some professors compare learning law to learning a new language. The experience of learning legal research certainly supports that analogy. The chapter's glossary anticipates terms that may be new to you, and gives you a place to turn back and refresh your memory if later in the chapter, or later in the book, terms don't make sense.

Next, each introductory chapter helps you understand what you find by explaining who or what created the source you found and the process followed in creating the authority. This part is called "You Have to Know How It's Made to Understand What You Are Seeing." For example, some of the sources you find online are the result of official authorship (that is, they were authorized by an official body of some kind) and some are not. Some sources are the actual text of the law created by legislators through established processes. Others, like committee reports, are an interesting byproduct of the legislative process. Some sources, like enacted statutes, must always be used as a basis for your analysis. But others may simply be helpful in your research and drafting and never appear in your final written work. Then, the introductory chapters move to setting out the basics about the particular source. The points made in this section may be short tips — information or illustrations about the source or how it relates or connects to other sources. Because the relationship among sources, changed by the context of each new issue or new fact scenario, is so important, you will likely find sidebars explaining and highlighting those connections.

The introductory chapter to a particular source then sets out an example that you can follow, step-by-step, to see how a researcher might approach a problem that involves the particular type of authority. Because we believe that you can't really understand a source until you understand how you will use it in predictive or persuasive reasoning expressed in writing, the chapter moves on to tell you how to write about and how to use the source. Finally, we follow the Examples and Explanations series practice of setting out "Examples," which are questions that ask you to apply what you've read in the chapter, and "Explanations," which are answers that help you to judge your choices. In some chapters, we ask open-ended research questions for which the answers may change with changing jurisdictions or time. The explanations for those questions will explain the things you are most likely to find, in most jurisdictions. The explanations will help you judge whether you found what you needed and whether the jurisdiction you chose is typical. Examples and Explanations are important both to check your understanding of what you read and to give you practice with the source.

The second, more advanced chapter in each pair of chapters on the three most important types of primary authorities focuses on different approaches you might adopt when undertaking research, and then on evaluating and using the authorities you find. Each of these advanced chapters includes examples — some simpler and others more complex — of research problems that you might encounter in practice. These examples walk you through the research process, showing how you might identify relevant authorities and assess their usefulness, how you should read an authority (what you should look out for; what parts are more or less important), and how authorities relate to one another.

The more advanced chapters end, as do most of the chapters in the book, with more examples and explanations. These examples may ask you to consider the relationship between different types of authorities, to take a problem and think about the research process you would use to address it, or to assess statements about authorities. Although there is no single "right" way to conduct research, some of the explanations will suggest a research process template that you might find helpful.

HOW TO USE THIS BOOK

Both common sense and learning theory influenced the way we structured the book, and we suggest that how you use it will directly affect how well you learn to become increasingly confident as you continue to practice legal research.

Three principles should guide the way you use this book: self-explanation, retrieval, and interleaving.[1]

Examples and Self-Explanation: Educational psychologists have studied how using examples can be a superior method of learning for beginners. For beginners, examples can lessen the "cognitive load," or mental energy necessary to complete a task of new learning. Critical to the process, however, is the concept of "self-explanation," or actively engaging and articulating for yourself the reasons supporting your choices. You might think of this as "putting it in your own words." Passive observation robs examples of their value. Thus, it's important for you to self-explain as you work through the examples and explanations at the end of each chapter. Verbalize why you chose an answer. Actively evaluate and reflect on your choices. Reflection extends your practice. Forcing yourself to stay engaged in this way will make your learning both deeper and more durable.

Retrieval: Many students assume that the best way to learn something is to read it over and over again until it feels etched on the brain. But studies show

---

1. If you would like to know more about retrieval and interleaving, we suggest reading *Make It Stick* by Peter C. Brown, Henry L. Roediger III, and Mark A. McDaniel (Harvard University Press 2014). If you would like to know more about cognitive load, see *Cognitive Load Theory*, by John Sweller and Paul Ayres (Springer 2011).

that retrieving information through self-testing is a far superior method of learning. It's counter-intuitive because practicing retrieval early means that often you are trying to remember things that you can't remember. It feels like you are failing. But in truth, it is the process — the act of retrieval — that produces far better learning. Thus, use the questions in the books to practice retrieval. In addition to using the Examples and Explanations questions at the end of the chapter, you can test yourself as you read by creating your own questions. For example, you might ask yourself to list the key points and how the main ideas relate to each other.

Interleaving: Educational psychologists discuss two kinds of practice, "massed practice" and "interleaving." In "massed practice," learners repeat the same thing over and over until they feel they have mastered it. It's a deceptive feeling, because massed practice results in learning that is not particularly long lasting. It's like cramming for a test, and then realizing a month later that you have lost that knowledge. In contrast, using "interleaving," where learners space out their practice and go back to it periodically after working with new topics, is more successful at later retrieving the information.

This principle counsels that as you use the book, you occasionally return to an earlier chapter to repeat just the Examples and Explanations from that earlier chapter. You'll be using both retrieval and interleaving if you do. Furthermore, interleaving is especially useful in law. One of the major themes of this book is that sources are connected, and that their usefulness varies, depending on the context. Interleaving will help you discover for yourself how legal sources work mainly in the changing connections among them. It will make your learning more successful and deepen your understanding of the law at the same time.

THE VARIABLES

How you approach a research problem depends on many things — the level of your substantive expertise in the area, the purposes of your research and what you expect to accomplish, the context of the problem you hope to answer, your familiarity with the different types of authorities that are important in the domain, the tools and resources available to you, and constraints like time and money. In every step of the research, analysis, and writing process you will be exercising judgment — which authorities are most relevant, what is their relative weight, how can they be used to further your client's interests — and that judgment can be developed through thoughtful and repeated practice. We hope that this book helps you to understand authorities, how they relate to one another, and how they are used, but it is only through practice that you will develop proficiency in research and become more efficient in the research, analysis, and writing process. And, remember, practice can be fun! There is something very rewarding about blazing a research trail, foraging, discovering bits and pieces of useful authority, and then gathering them together to build an argument or structure a transaction.

Remember as well that your research process will depend on the resources available to you and the circumstances in which you find yourself. If you are in the courtroom trying to counter an unanticipated argument from your opponent, or in a rural setting trying to answer questions from people who may never have had a chance to speak to a lawyer, you will need to think on the fly and adapt your research methods to the situations you face.

IN CONCLUSION

We emphasize that, like all your future research and writing, you should think about this book in the context of the relationships involved. Your professor is your guide for legal research. If the advice of this book conflicts with your professor's advice, please follow your professor!

Finally, research is a process of discovery. Discovering new information, integrating that information into our own cognition, and using it to help our clients and serve the rule of law makes us — and the people we serve — better. Although legal research can be confusing, and the resources and authorities intimidating, research — and then using the products of that research — is one of the most creative tasks that lawyers undertake. We are lucky because our jobs as students and lawyers — in whatever context we work — require that we stay engaged, learn new things, and change our ideas as the law and the practice of research changes. We wish you the considerable joy that understanding, finding, and using sources to create an argument or serve a client can bring.

Weight of Authority

Landscape with Irises, Henry Ossawa Tanner (1914)

Though you may hear me holler,
And you may see me cry —
I'll be dogged, sweet baby,
If you gonna see me die.
Life is fine! Fine as wine! Life is fine!

— Langston Hughes, *Life Is Fine*

Many of us have sat in high school or college classes where we talk and think about art, whether it's poetry or prose or sculpture or film, and discuss what it "means" and how we should interpret it. We can appreciate and enjoy a poem like *Life Is Fine* or a painting like Tanner's, and understand that art can enrich us simply by our experience of it. That experience is personal — it differs for all of us. What informs our appreciation depends on our own experiences and knowledge. But sometimes our involvement with art is deepened if we know something about the artist and the context in which she worked — what was going on in her life, in the time and location in which she lived, and in the artistic community in which she worked. We all bring to bear different knowledge and experiences in our interactions with art, and we all give more weight to some things than others as we engage with it. And the beauty of it is that there's no wrong or right way to experience art. Although artists learn rules of perspective, color, and composition, people who enjoy art remain largely unaware if the rules have been followed!

In some ways law is an art — lawyers have lots of discretion in choosing what arguments to make and how to structure transactions. That's what makes the practice and study of law challenging and interesting and, dare we say it, fun. But although we may not think much about the rules of composition when we look at a painting or read a poem, the legal reader is highly aware of the complex rules lawyers follow when deciding what authorities are relevant and how they should be used. Not all authorities are equal. Understanding and applying the complex rules of authority will help determine whether legal arguments will succeed. No matter how creative you are about crafting arguments, if you don't find the right authorities and apply them appropriately, you will lose your argument — or the advice you give to your client will come back to haunt him (and you).

Your clients will come to you with problems and plans. A single father wants to move out of state with his children and worries about whether their mother can object. A business owner wants to build on land that lies within a protected habitat. An employee wants to know whether her political activities can be held against her in the workplace.

As a lawyer, you will — and you must — look at your client's situation in light of the authorities that govern it. What you bring to bear on a client's problems or plans is dictated by what authorities apply and the relative strengths of those authorities. There are some authorities that you must apply, and there are others that you will have discretion to apply (or to argue that they should apply). Some authorities will serve as much stronger support for your position than others. Using authorities properly means recognizing their relative importance and strengths.

This isn't always easy. Think of all the law that exists. There are statutes and cases and regulations and administrative orders and court rules . . . and more! Even worse, all of those authorities are promulgated by both our federal system of government *and* the governments of our fifty states (not to mention rules and laws that localities pass and enforce). And that's just the actual law, only some — not all — of which must be applied to particular situations (that is to say, is mandatory). The good news is that there are relatively simple and easy to remember rules that help us evaluate authorities in relation to one another. But sometimes applying those rules gets a little tricky. This chapter will help you figure out what primary authorities apply in particular situations, how those authorities apply, and how authorities are balanced and weighed against each other.

GLOSSARY

Authority: A statement or discussion, usually about law, that lawyers use to support an assertion or argument.

Primary authority: The law itself. In our system, three branches of government promulgate laws — the legislature, the judiciary, and the executive. Each branch produces different types of laws, but in promulgating those laws, each branch must adhere to a well-defined process. Primary authorities are statements of law that are promulgated in accordance with the appropriate process and that are intended to be generally applicable and enforceable, or that apply to specific controversies or questions before the particular government body.

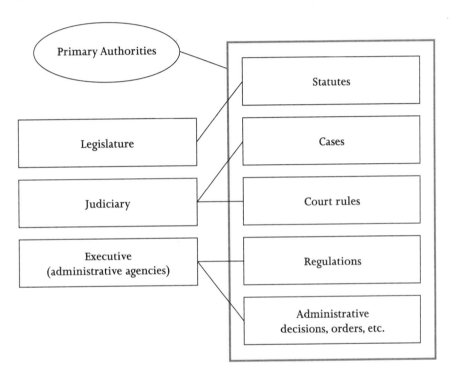

Secondary authority: When people write *about* the law (or about anything else, for that matter) they are writing secondary authority. Whether it's a law review article, a treatise, an "Examples and Explanations" volume (like this one!), a dictionary, an encyclopedia, a Wikipedia entry, a Twitter commentary, a blog post, or any of the many other kinds of texts written by individuals about the law, these texts are secondary authorities. Secondary sources — their usefulness, strengths, and weaknesses — are covered in Chapter 10.

Mandatory authority: Mandatory authority is a binding authority in a particular jurisdiction or context. If an authority is binding, the decision-maker must follow it. It controls a situation or set of facts.

42 U.S.C. § 2000e-2
(prohibits employers from
discriminating on the basis
of race, color, religion, sex,
or national origin).
MANDATORY AUTHORITY
ACROSS THE ENTIRE U.S.

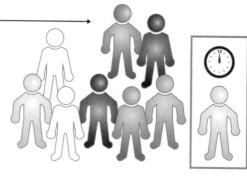

New York Consolidated
Laws, Labor Law, § 162
(requires that each person
working in a factory is entitled
to 60 minutes for lunch).
MANDATORY AUTHORITY
ONLY IN NEW YORK STATE.

N.Y. residents

Persuasive authority: An authority that is not mandatory, that can provide guidance but that does not control a set of facts. For example, the
decisions of the Supreme Court of California are not binding or mandatory
in Oregon. That is, a state or federal court in Oregon is not required to apply
the decision of a California court on a matter of Oregon law. But if you are
writing a brief to the Oregon Supreme Court on an issue which the Oregon
court has not addressed, you might cite the California Supreme Court case in
order to **persuade** the Oregon court that a particular outcome is appropriate.
The California Supreme Court case is, in this situation, a persuasive authority. (In a California court, it would be a mandatory authority.)

Decision: The outcome of a case. Sometimes the decision can be as short as
"Judgment for the plaintiff in the amount of $100,000." Or, the decision
may be conveyed in an opinion that is tens — or hundreds — of pages long.

Holding: The rule of law applied to the facts of the case before the court,
which sometimes changes the rule for future cases. The holding should be
distinguished from dicta that might be included in an opinion.

Dicta: Text in a court's opinion that is not essential to the holding in a
case. In writing opinions, judges often go on and on (often at great length!)
about the policies and reasoning behind their decisions, about what might
be the outcome of the case if the facts were different, about why the court
decided to hold as it did, or about anything else that might come to the

minds of the judges. The parts of an opinion that are not essential to — or do not state — the holding of the case are dicta. Statements of dicta are not binding on other courts.

Stare Decisis: The rule that a court should ordinarily follow the holdings of its own prior cases, as well as the mandate to harmonize new decisions with previous mandatory precedent from higher courts. *Stare decisis* is the rule of precedent. When a court decides a particular issue of law, it should, as a general rule, apply that same rule of law to future cases in which the same issue arises. The great majority of judicial decisions reflect the rule of precedent. But sometimes courts choose not to follow the rule articulated in earlier cases; perhaps they determine that the rule is no longer a good one, that circumstances have changed and the rule should no longer apply, or that the rule, in fact, violates the Constitution or certain statutes. Some of our most important decisions — like Brown v. Board of Education — reflect a decision by a court not to follow the rule of precedent.

THE BASICS YOU NEED TO KNOW

Primary authority can be either mandatory or persuasive, depending on the issue and the jurisdiction in which it is used or applied.

- In the jurisdiction in which it was enacted (legislation), promulgated (administrative regulations), or decided (case law), primary authority is mandatory.
- Outside of the jurisdiction in which it was enacted, promulgated, or decided, primary authority is only persuasive.

When we say an authority controls, we mean that it governs the situation and it is mandatory.

- So, in the State of Texas, the decisions of the Texas Supreme Court control in lower court cases in which similar issues arise. The Texas Revised Statutes and the Texas Administrative Code govern — and control — activities in the State of Texas.

You need to know these hierarchies of primary authority. They show the most powerful authority at the top, which always trumps those below. Memorize these and think about how to apply them. Use them to choose which authorities to use, and how to structure your argument.

Hierarchy of law from various branches of government within one jurisdiction.

(This chart assumes that each source is properly created and constitutional.)

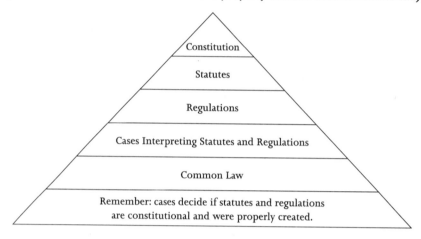

Hierarchy within a jurisdiction's court system.

(This chart assumes each court properly had jurisdiction to decide the case.)

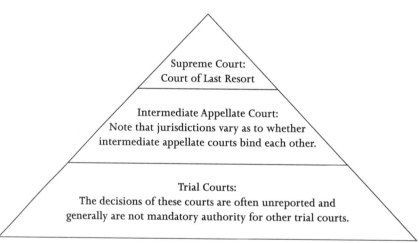

Within the jurisdiction in which they were enacted, statutes are always mandatory authority.

- Statutes enacted by the U.S. Congress are mandatory authority across the United States.
- Statutes enacted by a state's legislature are mandatory authority in that state.

Connections: Illinois law — statutes, regulations, and cases — is mandatory in Illinois. Suppose that an automobile accident occurs in Ohio, but, because at least some of the injured persons live in Chicago, the case for damages is being tried in an Illinois state court. The Illinois court may determine to apply Ohio law to some of the issues that come before it because that is where the accident occurred (this is a choice of law question). If the Illinois court decides that Ohio law applies, the Illinois court will look to Ohio statutes, cases, and regulations as mandatory authority (although ordinarily Ohio law is not at all mandatory authority in Illinois).

Illinois judge   Car wreck in Ohio

↓

Ohio cases, statutes, and regulations

Within the jurisdiction in which they are promulgated, regulations adopted by administrative agencies are mandatory authority.

- Regulations promulgated by federal administrative agencies (e.g., the Environmental Protection Agency, the Internal Revenue Service, and the Department of Labor) are mandatory authority across the United States.
- Regulations promulgated by a state administrative agency (e.g., the Delaware Department of Labor, the Georgia Forestry Commission, the North Dakota Beef Commission, and the Hawaii Department of Transportation) are mandatory authority within that state.

If a statute in a jurisdiction conflicts with a regulation in that same jurisdiction, the statute controls.

- Administrative agencies get their authority from the legislature (lots more about this in Chapter 7). When it adopts a regulation, an agency cannot exceed the authority granted to it by the legislature, nor can its regulations conflict with existing statutes.

Statutes outweigh individual court decisions.

- Unless a court finds that a statute violates the Constitution (or that a state statute violates that state's constitution), the court must apply the statute as written. Even the U.S. Supreme Court is bound by the text of constitutional federal statutes.

The holdings of the highest level court in a jurisdiction are mandatory authority in that jurisdiction.

- The holdings of the U.S. Supreme Court are mandatory authority across the country.
- The holdings of the highest court in each state are mandatory authority within that state.
- The U.S. Supreme Court (and other courts as well) can find that the laws of any state (as passed by the legislature, as enunciated by the judiciary, or as promulgated by administrative agencies) are contrary to the United States Constitution and, therefore, invalid.

Lower courts in a particular jurisdiction are bound by the decisions of higher courts in the same jurisdiction.

- In our federal system, all lower courts — from federal district courts, to bankruptcy courts, to circuit courts of appeals — are bound by the decisions of the U.S. Supreme Court.
- Lower federal courts (e.g., federal district courts) are also bound by the decisions of the court of appeals in the circuit in which the lower court is located. So, for example, the federal district court for the Southern District of New York is bound by the decisions of the Second Circuit Court of Appeals. The federal district court for the Southern District of New York is not required to follow the decisions of any other federal circuit court of appeals. But note that this is the rule for the federal courts — it may not be the rule in state court systems.

Connections: An appellate court may or may not have to follow the decisions of other appellate courts in its jurisdiction. In our federal system, one circuit court of appeals need not follow the decisions in another court of appeals.

Question (in federal court): Can X do Y?

2d Circuit (1998): Yes!	5th Circuit (2005): No!

But in some state court systems, the decisions of one appellate court bind other appellate courts at the same level.

Question (in California state court): Can A do B in California?

California 1st District Court of Appeals (2002): Yes!

All other California district courts of appeals must also answer: Yes!

The lesson? Know the rules that apply in your jurisdiction!

The doctrine of precedent (stare decisis) suggests that courts in a single jurisdiction follow the holdings of earlier cases decided by higher courts in the jurisdiction.

- Dicta is persuasive authority only. It's the holding that controls.

The higher the court, the stronger the authority.

- Cases decided by the highest court in a jurisdiction are stronger authorities than the decisions of intermediate appellate courts in that jurisdiction.

A case that addresses a relevant issue, and that has facts similar to the facts of your case, is a stronger authority than a case decided by the same court on the same issue, but with very different facts.

Sometimes there is no mandatory authority that governs a particular issue.

- You will sometimes find that a particular question of law has never before been addressed in your jurisdiction. In that case, you will have to base your argument entirely on a persuasive authority that you determine should control the resolution of your issue.

Secondary authority is never mandatory.

- Secondary authorities are not law, and so they can only be persuasive (at best — some secondary authorities may not be very persuasive at all!).
- Secondary authorities can never, ever control.

Secondary authorities differ greatly among themselves and serve different purposes.

- Secondary sources are written for practitioners, students, scholars, and the public (Chapter 10 goes into great detail about the different uses and relative strengths of secondary authorities).
- Some secondary sources (like legal encyclopedias, for example) should rarely — if ever — be used in making an argument before a court or an administrative agency, while other secondary sources (e.g., law review articles) can be very useful in making policy and other types of arguments before courts and other governing bodies.

  Experienced attorneys are more likely to use sources written by an identifiable and prestigious author.

HOW IT WORKS: AN EXAMPLE

When entrepreneurs start a business, they usually choose to form an entity through which the business is operated. By doing so, and by following their jurisdiction's statutes governing business entities, entrepreneurs can avoid individual responsibility for the debts and other liabilities of the business. Entrepreneurs could choose to form a general partnership, a limited partnership, a corporation, a limited liability company, or any of the many other business entities authorized by the statutes of the state in which they choose to form their business.

Some of these forms of business entities — like corporations and partnerships — have been around for a long time. Statutes governing corporations have existed for hundreds of years and, since corporations get into as much trouble as any of us, in most jurisdictions there are many cases (hundreds or thousands) that have considered questions about corporations. In fact, savvy business owners often choose to form corporations in Delaware because that state has so much case law on corporations. Because of that common law tradition, business owners who form corporations in Delaware have some certainty about how corporate problems will be resolved in the courts. And because businesses hate uncertainty, they like Delaware. Because of the Delaware courts' expertise when it comes to corporations, many other states' courts look to Delaware court decisions for guidance, and as persuasive authority when similar questions arise in their own jurisdictions.

But suppose your client, Lilly Lou Conroe, chose not to form a corporation (which brings with it lots of requirements, formalities, and expense), but instead formed one of the newer, more flexible, and less expensive kinds of business entities created specifically for smaller businesses. Lilly formed a limited liability company (or LLC) and she formed that company in the State of Nevada.

As creatures of statute, LLCs came into being relatively recently (i.e., in the last several years), and consequently, there have been far fewer opportunities for courts to consider questions about LLCs. There's not a whole lot of case law in any jurisdiction on LLCs.

So now Lilly and her LLC are in trouble. A creditor of the LLC has sued Lilly individually, claiming that she should be liable for the debts of the LLC because she managed it as her own business, and not as a separate entity.

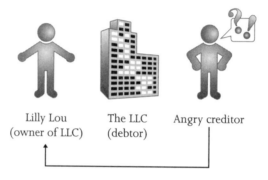

Lilly Lou   The LLC   Angry creditor
(owner of LLC)   (debtor)

Where should you start your research to determine whether Lilly might be individually liable? You might well want to start with a secondary source to learn a little bit about LLCs. But once you know the lay of the land, what primary authority would you turn to first? That's easy — **always start with the statute**. The Nevada statute that authorizes the formation of LLCs and dictates how they are to be organized and managed should be your first stop. The statute is a mandatory authority. But suppose that the statute — which sets forth general rules and cannot deal with specific facts — does not answer the question of whether Lilly's behavior makes her individually liable.

Your next step would be to look for Nevada case law that might be relevant. Sadly, Nevada courts have not addressed this question. If they had and if the Nevada Supreme Court had considered a similar question, its decision would control Lilly's situation and you would likely need to look no further. But there's no relevant Nevada case law. Now what?

You expand your research. For Lilly's problem, you could expand your research in two different ways — across contexts, and across jurisdictions. First, you could look for authorities in Nevada that address a similar issue in a slightly different context. There might be Nevada case law that answers the question of whether someone who operated a *corporation* (rather than an LLC) would be individually liable if she acted like Lilly did. Or, you could look for authorities in *other jurisdictions* that also have LLCs to see if an issue like Lilly's has ever arisen there.

If you found any of these authorities, they would be persuasive, rather than mandatory. Any Nevada cases you find that address Lilly's issue in the context of a corporation would certainly be useful, but since it's a different statute that the court interpreted, those cases do not control Lilly's situation. And cases from other jurisdictions, interpreting their own LLC statute (which may or may not be similar to Nevada's), can never be binding on a Nevada court that interprets Nevada law.

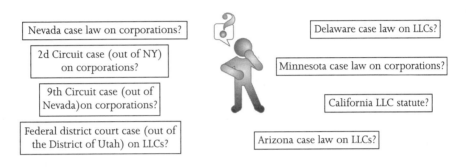

Let's say that you found the following authorities that address the issue of whether Lilly might be liable in similar — but not identical — situations:

- A 2011 decision of the Nevada Supreme Court that considers a similar question in the context of corporations, rather than LLCs. The facts are somewhat different from Lilly's situation.
- A 2014 decision from an intermediate Minnesota appellate court with a very similar fact pattern and a similar question, but in the context of a corporation.
- A provision in the California LLC statute that would answer the question of whether Lilly is individually liable.
- A 2001 decision by the 9th Circuit Court of Appeals interpreting the Nevada statute on corporations in a case with facts slightly different from Lilly's.
- A 2013 decision by the federal district court for the District of Utah construing the Utah LLC statute (which is nearly identical to that of Nevada's) in a case with facts very similar to Lilly's.
- A 2015 decision from the 2d Circuit Court of Appeals interpreting the New York corporations statute in a case with a very different fact pattern.
- A 2000 decision from the Arizona Supreme Court interpreting its LLC statute (which is not so similar to Nevada's) in a case with a very different fact pattern from Lilly's.
- A 2015 case decided by Delaware's Court of Chancery interpreting Delaware's corporations statute in a case with a nearly identical fact

pattern. (The Delaware Court of Chancery is the trial court in Delaware that considers corporations-related questions.)

Think about the strengths and weaknesses of each of these authorities in their application to Lilly's problem in Nevada. What would make one of these authorities more or less persuasive than the others?

Generally, the higher the court, the stronger the authority. But here we're balancing (i) cases from the highest courts in a couple of jurisdictions against (ii) a lower court decision in a jurisdiction that is known for its corporate law expertise against (iii) decisions of high level federal appellate courts. We can't just look at the highest level of court and decide that its decision is the most persuasive. We need to think about a lot of factors. What about the age of the decision? The age of a case can work both ways — if a statute is frequently amended, a more recent case might be more persuasive. If the statute is a long standing one and the case interpreting it has been very frequently cited by other courts as stating the rule in the state, then the older case might be a better authority.

We also need to think about geography, demographics, and culture. Would you expect Nevada to be more likely to share the policies and approach of states like Arizona and Utah or New York and Delaware? And, maybe most importantly in Lilly's case, how similar are the statutes that the courts are interpreting? If a state's statute is very different from Nevada, it won't matter that the highest court in the state decided the issue, or that the fact pattern was very similar.

Finally, how does the court treat the issue? Does the court analyze the issue and discuss relevant authorities in some depth, or is the court's treatment of the issue more cursory, without much analysis? The more in-depth the analysis, the stronger the authority.

So, let's look again at our authorities:

- A 2011 decision of the Nevada Supreme Court that considers a similar question in the context of corporations, rather than LLCs. The facts are significantly different from Lilly's situation.

Strengths	Weaknesses
The highest court in Nevada	It's not the LLC statute
Construing a Nevada statute that is at least related to the LLC statute	Facts are different
Relatively recent	
Policies ought to be the same whether it's a corporations question or an LLC question	

- A 2014 decision from an intermediate Minnesota appellate court with a very similar fact pattern and a similar question, but in the context of a corporation.

Strengths	Weaknesses
Recent	It's only an intermediate appellate court
Facts are similar	In a state that is very different from Nevada
	Not an LLC, but a corporation (and we don't know if Minnesota's corporations statute is similar to Nevada's)

- A provision in the California LLC statute that would answer the question of whether Lilly is individually liable.

Strengths	Weaknesses
	It's a different statute from Nevada's. A California statute doesn't help us interpret a Nevada statute

- A 2001 decision by the 9th Circuit Court of Appeals interpreting the Nevada corporations statute in a case with facts slightly different from Lilly's.

Strengths	Weaknesses
A high level federal appellate court	The 9th Circuit is less of an authority when it comes to Nevada law than the Nevada Supreme Court
Construing a Nevada statute that is at least related to the LLC statute	Facts are different
The 9th Circuit ought to have significant expertise when it comes to Nevada law (because Nevada is in the 9th Circuit).	Relatively old case (Has it been frequently cited? Has the Nevada Supreme Court ever cited it?)
Facts are only slightly different	It's the corporations statute, not the LLC statute
Policies ought to be the same whether it's a corporation question or an LLC question	

- A 2013 decision by the federal district court for the District of Utah construing the Utah LLC statute (which is nearly identical to that of Nevada's) in a case with facts very similar to Lilly's.

Strengths	Weaknesses
It's an LLC statute that's being interpreted	It's a trial court (the lowest level of court)
Utah's LLC statute is very similar to Nevada's	It's Utah, not Nevada
Relatively recent	
Facts are very similar	
Nevada is close to Utah in geography and demographics and, at least to some extent, culture	

- A 2015 decision from the Court of Appeals for the Second Circuit interpreting the New York corporations statute in a case with a very different fact pattern.

Strengths	Weaknesses
It's a high level federal appellate court	It's not the LLC statute (and who knows if NY's corporations statute has much in common with Nevada's?)
Recent	It's New York, not Nevada, and New York doesn't have a whole lot in common with Nevada
	Very different facts

- A 2000 decision from the Arizona Supreme Court interpreting its LLC statute (which is not so similar to Nevada's) in a case with a very different fact pattern from Lilly's.

Strengths	Weaknesses
The highest court in Arizona	It's Arizona, not Nevada
Nevada and Arizona are pretty close in geography, demographics, and culture — perhaps they share the same policies and the same approach to businesses	Arizona's LLC statute is very different from Nevada's
	Facts are very different
	Case is relatively old (but it might be the leading case on the issue and, so, might be frequently cited)

- A 2015 case decided by Delaware's Court of Chancery interpreting Delaware's corporations statute in a case with a nearly identical fact pattern. (The Delaware Court of Chancery is the trial court in Delaware that considers corporations-related questions.)

Strengths	Weaknesses
Delaware courts have a lot of expertise when it comes to business entities	It's a trial court
Recent case	Interpreting a corporations statute (not an LLC statute)
Nearly identical fact pattern	Delaware is likely a lot different from Nevada in culture and demographics (but it might be more similar in its approach to business)

In a real world scenario, you are likely to find far more than eight authorities that might be relevant to your issue. And it will be hard, if not impossible, to list those authorities from strongest to least useful. But you should be able to make some generalizations about their relative strengths that will help you determine how best to use them. For our eight authorities, it's safe to say that:

- The California statute is not useful.
- The Minnesota and New York cases are not particularly useful either. We don't know much about those states' corporations statutes and their similarity — or lack thereof — to Nevada's, and there's not a lot of connection between Minnesota or New York and Nevada.
- The Arizona Supreme Court case is a little better, but not much. Arizona's LLC statute is very different from Nevada's, so to the extent that the Arizona court's decision rests on the language of the Arizona statute, its decision becomes less relevant. But if the court's decision is not tied to the language of the statute, but rather is grounded in common law, the case might be persuasive. And it might be especially persuasive if the Arizona Supreme Court discussed the issue in great detail and described its reasoning in reaching its decision.
- The Delaware Chancery Court case might be used to support your argument (although trial court decisions are not, as a general rule, particularly persuasive). Delaware and Nevada, although very different states, share a certain business orientation. If the Chancery Court adopted an approach and reasoning that supported Lilly's position, you could cite the Delaware decision to buttress your argument, pointing out the expertise of the Chancery Court and acknowledging the fact that the Delaware court was interpreting the corporations statute and not the LLC statute. This argument works

only if the Delaware court's decision does not hinge on the exact text of the statute.

- The Nevada Supreme Court case, the 9th Circuit decision, and the federal district court case in Utah are all relatively strong authorities. The Utah case, although decided by a trial court, interprets an LLC statute very similar to Nevada's in the context of a fact situation that is nearly identical to Lilly's. If the court discusses the issue at any length, the opinion could be very helpful to you in sorting out Lilly's problem. Both the 9th Circuit opinion and the Nevada Supreme Court opinion interpret the Nevada corporations statute. The rationales of those courts in resolving a similar issue may well apply to Lilly's situation. The Nevada Supreme Court is, of course, the ultimate arbiter when it comes to Nevada law, and so, has greater expertise than the 9th Circuit on Nevada law. On the other hand, the facts of the case considered by the 9th Circuit are more similar to Lilly's. Any or all of these three cases could be used effectively to support an argument or outcome in Lilly's case.

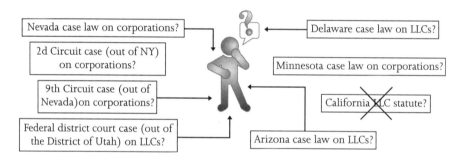

WRITING ABOUT AUTHORITIES

Understanding how you will write about authorities will help you understand the value of the sources you find, and the connections among sources as you research. You'll find more advice and reminders about individual types of sources in the chapters devoted to those particular sources. Here, we'll look in an introductory way at some of the ways you can organize your writing to signal that you understand legal analysis and have taken the weight of authority into account as you write. Further, the language you use can show your reader you understand the value of the sources you cite.

1. *Weight of authority principles will usually determine the order in which you present sources to the reader.* Often you will be tempted to start your analysis with a source that provides the opportunity to make the

arguments you want to make, regardless of its precedential value. This would be a mistake. Instead, you should almost always let weight of authority principles guide your organization. Start with the mandatory authority — often a relevant statute or, in the absence of a statute on point, a relevant case from your jurisdiction. You'll analyze the rule from the statute or case to form an outline of your paper. If you are working with a statute, for each part of the statute at issue, you'll start with the text of the statute, and then move to mandatory case law interpreting the statute. If no statute is involved, you'll start with the mandatory case law that sets out your rule. When setting out cases within the discussion of a particular issue or sub-issue, you'll start with mandatory authority, even if it doesn't determine the outcome of your case.

For more on specific ways to organize your discussion, see your legal writing textbook or the materials provided by your teacher. You can also check the chapters in this book devoted to specific sources. In the LLC problem above, even if you didn't find the statute first, it's the source you would *use first* when writing your analysis.

2. *Weight of authority principles will sometimes determine the amount of space you give to sources.* In addition to showing that you understand how weight of authority operates by the order in which you present authorities, with the strongest coming first, you should think about the amount of space that you devote to each source. It's a subtle signal to your reader about how important you think the source is. A few examples:

If you had two mandatory cases, and one had facts more similar to your case, you would describe the case with similar facts in more depth and at greater length than the other.

If you found a mandatory case that wasn't very helpful, and a persuasive case that helped a lot, even though you would discuss the mandatory case first, you might devote more space to the persuasive case.

If you found a primary authority on a point that wasn't very helpful, and a good secondary source discussing the issue, you would still put the primary authority first. You might, however, discuss the secondary source at more length. This example will occur rarely. In your first-year classes, professors will often discourage the use of secondary authority in your practice-oriented documents.

Further, you have several choices about whether to include details about the case. It's often helpful to include enough factual context to know what the case concerned, but sometimes a parenthetical is all you will need to describe the case. If the case is a linchpin of your analysis, you'll want to include the details in the text. And if you haven't found an authority that can serve as a linchpin, you might want to keep looking.

3. *Whether a source is mandatory will determine the language you use writing about that source.* Remember that the court has a duty to follow the law established within constitutional bounds by the legislature or by higher courts. But the court has no obligation to consider other sources no matter how persuasive they are. Be careful to choose language that reflects whether the source is mandatory or persuasive. You always want to be careful about telling the court that it "must" do something, because the mix of law and facts is usually a matter of interpretation. But it may be appropriate to use "must" with primary, mandatory authority that is squarely relevant. It is rarely appropriate when your support is a persuasive source. You might instead write that the court should "consider" or "may be persuaded."

4. *Whether a source is primary or secondary may determine the language you use writing about that source.* Similar to the guideline for choosing language that reflects whether a source is mandatory or persuasive authority, you should be careful to avoid writing about secondary authority as if you were writing about the law. Secondary authority is persuasive at best, and sometimes hardly that.

5. *The same factors that went into your decision about how much weight to give an authority will also apply to the way you write about the source, especially when you write as an advocate. You will emphasize the aspects of the case that are similar to your case.* When you are learning to write about authority, it is easy to fall into the habit of setting out each source in a paragraph that is always structured the same way. We learn default organizations, such as IRAC, that encourage novices to rely on one formula that usually works. Knowing this default organization can help students face new situations. Novices automatically set out the rule, the facts of the precedent, and the rationale of the court in reaching the rule. Each paragraph illustrating or explaining the law looks and feels very much like the other paragraphs in length and detail. This makes it harder for the reader to know instinctively which sources are key to the analysis. Instead, consider letting your reader know up front why you have chosen the case — either by beginning with a carefully crafted topic sentence or by varying how much emphasis you give to each part of explaining the case. If you chose the case because it has facts similar to your case, emphasize the facts of the precedent. If you chose it for the rationale the court applied, condense the facts and write more about the rationale. Help your reader focus on what you want to take from the case. Don't hide the reason you chose to include it.

EXAMPLES AND EXPLANATIONS

Examples

1. Assume you are practicing in a Colorado trial court on a question of state environmental law that does not implicate the U.S. Constitution or the Colorado Constitution. You find a case from the United States Supreme Court on a different environmental issue involving a federal statute; a Colorado Supreme Court case interpreting another Colorado statute that also applies; and the Colorado environmental statute that the case interprets. Evaluate the following statements:

   A. You are not likely to find a United States Supreme Court opinion that is relevant.
   B. If you did find a Colorado statute and a United States Supreme Court opinion that you could apply, you would discuss the Colorado statute after discussing the United States Supreme Court case.
   C. You should set out the Colorado statute before you set out the Colorado Supreme Court case that addresses the statute.

2. You are given the following types of authorities for a writing assignment involving a federal issue, filed in a federal district court, within the geographical jurisdiction of the United States Court of Appeals for the 5th Circuit.

   (1) A case from the 5th Circuit that addresses the same issue, but whose facts are very different from your case.
   (2) A case from the Southern District of New York, but with facts almost identical to yours.
   (3) A case from the 9th Circuit with facts very similar to yours.
   (4) The federal statute involved in your case.
   (5) A case from the 5th Circuit with facts somewhat similar to yours.
   (6) A case from the United States Supreme Court that addresses your statute and issue, but is focused on policy, and not how the rule might apply to facts.

   How will you order the authorities and allocate the space you give them in your writing assignment? Evaluate the following suggestions:

   A. Put the federal statute first and then order cases and allocate space based on how similar the facts are to our case.
   B. Put the United States Supreme Court case first because it is the most powerful court, then the cases from the 5th Circuit, then the statute, and finally the cases from other jurisdictions.
   C. Put the federal statute first; then order the cases starting with the United States Supreme Court case, giving it the most space; then the cases from the 5th Circuit, giving them equal space; next would be the 9th Circuit

case; and finally, the case from the federal district court. Neither of the out-of-jurisdiction cases should take up much space.

D. Put the 5th Circuit case with similar facts first, then the United States Supreme Court case, then the other 5th Circuit case, and then the statute before the out-of-jurisdiction cases. Give nearly the same space to all the cases, because none of them are that much stronger than the others.

3. The highest court in your jurisdiction writes the following in a majority opinion: "Thus, Plaintiff's claim fails on the fourth element and therefore Plaintiff does not have a cause of action. Plaintiff might have shown the element by offering evidence such as a signed declaration of intent to purchase, but there was no such showing here." Answer the following questions about the opinion:

A. Can you use the case to show the first, second, and third elements, because the court said it was only the fourth element that failed?

B. Is this observation dicta or part of the holding: "The plaintiff might have shown the element by offering evidence such as a signed declaration of intent to purchase . . ."?

C. Can you use what the court said about element four to support an argument in a new case?

4. You are working on a case brought to federal court, and you've found an administrative regulation that you think is key to your analysis of the issue. Evaluate the following statements:

A. The regulation is primary authority.

B. The regulation is binding in your case.

C. The regulation would also be binding if the case were in state court instead.

D. You should find and analyze the federal statute that gave the agency the power to make the regulation.

E. The regulation is likely to be highly persuasive in your case.

Explanations

1. **A.** Although it is not impossible that you could find a helpful case from the United States Supreme Court, it would be unlikely. Assuming you found a U.S. Supreme Court case, it would be persuasive and not mandatory authority. To be useful, it would need to interpret a statutory provision or phrase worded exactly like the Colorado statute. Even then, you would first set out the Colorado statute and Colorado case law interpreting it. **B.** As observed above, in a case involving state law, you would set out the Colorado law before turning to the federal law. **C.** The text of the statute binds the court, so you would first set out the statute, and then the cases interpreting it.

2. You have a lot to balance in making choices in this example, and there may be more than one good way to order sources and allocate space. But some answers are better than others: **A.** Putting the statute first is a good choice, but to order the cases based only on how similar the facts are to your case would most likely confuse your legal reader. More likely you would order the authorities by highest to lowest, in terms of their place in the hierarchy of authority, and then go on to persuasive authority. You might use factual similarity to decide how much detail to include about the sources, but you will often look at the court's rationale or policy arguments. **B.** Although starting with the United States Supreme Court is tempting because we think of it as the most powerful, you should start by quoting the relevant parts of the statute. After setting out the statute, then you could go to the United States Supreme Court and the relevant 5th Circuit cases. Then to out-of-jurisdiction cases, probably starting with the 9th Circuit and finally the trial level court. **C.** This is probably the most sensible ordering of authority. But deciding not to give much space to out-of-jurisdiction cases may be problematic. If the facts of the case from the federal district court are truly very similar, you could decide to devote substantial space to it. This would especially be true if the facts are unusual or haven't often been addressed before. It is a common pattern for the analysis to be more fact-specific at the federal trial court level, and that can make those cases valuable choices. **D.** As we noted above, the best choice is to start with the statute. Next you would probably move to the United States Supreme Court. Remember that giving the same amount of space or detail to all the cases wastes the opportunity to signal to your reader the importance of the case to your analysis.

3. **A.** You cannot make any assumptions about the other elements. The court's silence does not mean that the elements are proven or not proven. The court has said the case fails on the fourth element. If the court had analyzed the fourth element more closely than the others, and found the case proven, then you could make assumptions about every element. But when it is unproven, you cannot assume anything about the other elements. **B.** This is dicta. Because it assumes facts that are not actually present in the case, it is a speculation about what the court would do if those facts were present. It is not part of the rule or holding. **C.** Yes. This is part of the holding and it becomes a mandatory precedent for your case.

4. **A.** Yes. The regulation is primary authority and thus is the law. **B.** Assuming the regulation is federal, properly created under the power of the enabling statute, and relevant, yes, it would be binding in a federal court. **C.** If it is a federal regulation and it applies to the facts before the court, it will still be mandatory authority, no matter if the case is heard in state or federal court. **D.** Yes. You should check the enabling statute. **E.** The regulation would be binding and not merely persuasive.

Identifying, Reading, Understanding, and Writing About Legislation

Paper airplanes controlled by smartphones. A locked wallet that opens only upon recognizing its owner's fingerprints. An instant jolt of caffeine in an energy spray for your skin. Entrepreneurs think up crazy and not-so-crazy products every day, with the hopes of sharing innovation and making a fortune. Only the best connected of those entrepreneurs have access to the kinds of funds that could make those dreams come true. It takes money to make a product, market it, and get it to the people who want it.

One way to finance a new product might be for the entrepreneur to form a corporation and sell shares to big and small investors. State statutes dictate how corporations are formed and how they operate. Federal securities laws — like the Securities Act of 1933 — have historically prevented companies from selling shares of stock to the public without going through the very expensive and time-consuming process of registering the stock and obtaining the approval of the Securities and Exchange Commission, a federal agency. With limited funds and no connection to big money, what's an entrepreneur to do?

The advent of crowdfunding sites on the Internet — like Kickstarter, Indiegogo, and Tilt — gave entrepreneurs a new way of funding their dreams. Fledgling business owners could solicit funds from the public in exchange for as little benefit as the satisfaction of contributing to a neat idea. Or donors might receive gifts from the entrepreneur in appreciation for their contributions — for example, the donor to the crowdfunding site might receive the smartphone app that controls the paper airplane, a sample of the energy spray, or a discount on the purchase of the wallet (if it's ever produced).

Many people — including legislators — thought we should be doing more to encourage this kind of creative, entrepreneurial endeavor. America was built on new ideas, and entrepreneurial success is good for the economy. Surely we'd want to minimize the burdens on entrepreneurs and ease the fundraising process. As crowdfunding took off, Congress recognized its potential to spur and support innovation. Accordingly, in 2013,

Congress amended the Securities Act of 1933 to allow — in defined and limited circumstances — sales of unregistered shares of stock to the public on crowdfunded websites.

Until 2013, federal legislation completely prohibited this activity, and now a federal statute expressly allows and even encourages it . . . in certain circumstances. Clients will want to take advantage of these new fundraising opportunities, and it's your job as lawyers to help them do that. You will need to understand the newly enacted legislation and how it relates to the laws already on the books. And you'll need to find clues as to how it should be interpreted. This chapter will help you understand how legislation is interpreted and applied, and how you can best write about legislation and its effects. The chapter begins by introducing you to the process by which new statutes come into being and how they relate to existing legislation. And then we'll give some examples of how we should — and should not — write about legislation. We'll get back to our smartphone-controlled paper airplane later.

GLOSSARY

Bills: Laws proposed by a member to a legislature.
Codify: To arrange by topic into a code.
Public Laws: Bills passed by Congress and approved by the President. As bills are enacted and approved, they are chronologically assigned.
Public Law Numbers: Numbers assigned to enacted bills that reflect the session of Congress in which they were passed.
Session Laws: All the Public Laws passed during a session of Congress.
Statutes: The term we most frequently use to describe enacted legislation.

YOU NEED TO KNOW HOW IT'S MADE TO UNDERSTAND WHAT YOU ARE SEEING

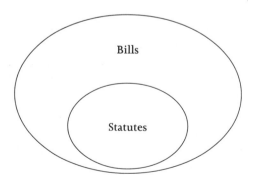

Bills are drafts of the laws **proposed** by a member of a legislative body to a legislature. In the federal system, bills are identified with sequential numbering, with an initial letter indicating whether the bill was introduced in the Senate (S) or the House of Representatives (HR). Many — if not most — bills introduced in a legislative session are never enacted by the legislature.

Statutes are bills that have been passed by the legislature and approved by the executive.

As bills are enacted by Congress, they are assigned **Public Law** numbers. Those numbers (e.g., Public Law 107-56) reflect the session of Congress in which the law was passed (the 107th) and its order in the chronology of all Public Laws passed during that legislative session (Public Law 107-56 was the 56th public law passed during the 107th session of Congress).

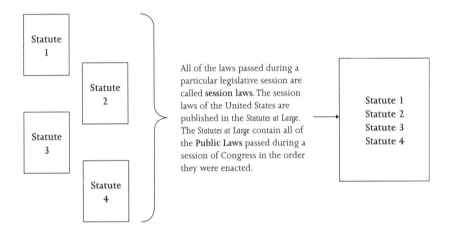

Most of your research on legislation will be done in what we call **codes** or codifications or codified statutes. Remember, session laws are published chronologically. The legislature then organizes the laws analytically — into subject-matter categories. Session laws often contain introductions (called "preambles") that describe the purposes of the legislation. That introductory text, because it provides context for the actual laws that follow and does not itself establish binding authority, is usually not codified. Moreover, the references within session laws are sometimes to the session law itself. When laws are codified, extraneous, nonbinding text is often deleted, and cross-references amended so that they refer to other provisions within the code.

When we talk about codes in a legislative context, we're talking about *all of a jurisdiction's currently effective legislation, arranged by subject.* Codes are updated as new legislation is enacted to reflect new laws, changes in existing laws, and repeals of laws. The United States Code is the codification of federal legislation. The United States Code is divided into smaller parts.

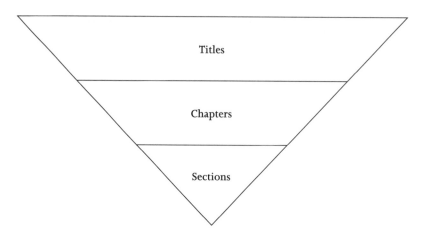

A title is a subject-specific part of a code. The United States Code is divided into 54 titles — each title contains federal laws relating to a particular topic. For example, Title 42 of the United States Code is on the topic of "The Public Health and Welfare." Statutes codified in Title 28 of the United States Code are all on the topic of "Judiciary and Judicial Procedure."

Titles of a code may be further subdivided into chapters (as are the titles of the United States Code). For example, debtors may file for bankruptcy under either Chapter VII or Chapter XIV of Title 11 of the U.S. Code. Which chapter the debtor uses dictates how the two different types of bankruptcy proceedings take place.

A section within a code is what we normally cite to when we refer to a law. Titles and chapters are divided into hundreds and sometimes thousands of sections. Each section is a statement of law, and often one section relates to those that closely precede and follow it.

State codes, like the United States Code, are divided into smaller parts too, but those smaller parts might not follow the title/chapter/section nomenclature. For example, the codified statutes in Texas are divided into several mini-codes (like the Penal Code, the Tax Code, the Family Code, and the Alcoholic Beverage Code); whatever subjects of legislation don't fit into the mini-codes are collected into something called the "Civil Statutes," which are further organized by topic.

Remember that you will use citations to identify a particular source, and that the citation lets the reader evaluate the weight of the authority you are using. The citation 42 U.S.C. §1983 refers to section 1983 of title 42 of the United States Code.

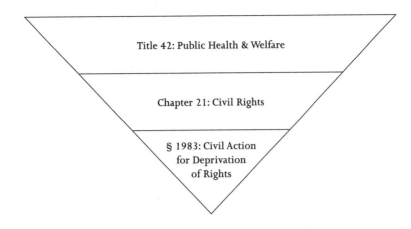

Title 42: Public Health & Welfare

Chapter 21: Civil Rights

§ 1983: Civil Action
for Deprivation
of Rights

THE BASICS YOU NEED TO KNOW

Connections: Statutes are mandatory authority and outweigh individual court decisions. Unless a court finds that a statute violates the Constitution (or that a state statute violates that state's constitution), the court *must* apply the statute as written.

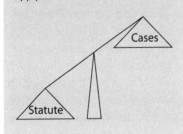

Most of what we do is governed by statute.

- Whether it's something as fundamental as who can marry, as simple as what counts as a burglary, or as complex as how we form a business, what taxes we pay, or how our parents' Social Security and Medicaid benefits are distributed, most of our activities and the nation's economy are governed by state or federal statutes.

In beginning your research, you should think about whether a state or federal statute, or both, might apply to your problem.

- The United States Code applies throughout the United States, and each of the states' codes is binding within that jurisdiction.

Most litigation that involves statutes relates to the interpretation and application of the statutory text.

- Unless there is a claim that a statute violates the United States Constitution or a state constitution, courts work **within the text of a statute**, trying to determine how its provisions apply to a particular set of facts.

You will usually need to find and apply the current, codified version of the statute.

Connections: Statutes are written so that they will apply to many different sets of facts. A court decision applies only to the case before the court. The rule of law established by a statute is more general and more widely applicable than the rule that emerges from a court decision.

Connections: For some important federal laws (as well as some state laws) that address specific areas of activity, it's easy to find citations to particular statutes — using either Google or tools within commercial databases — if you know the popular name of the legislation.

If you Google "Endangered Species Act citation" or search for "Endangered Species Act" in the popular name table of a commercial research database, you will quickly learn that the legislation is codified in sections 1531 through 1544 of Chapter 35 ("Endangered Species") of Title 16 ("Conservation") of the United States Code.

Connections: Statutes and administrative regulations have a special relationship: regulations govern implementation of the statute. And a certain kind of statute, an "enabling statute," gives life to regulations. When working with statutes, be on the lookout for related regulations.

- Unless your research project focuses on the history of legislation or involves an event that happened in the past, you do not need to refer to session laws or the text of laws as passed by the legislature. Instead, **you should review and cite to the codified versions of federal and state statutes, as those contain the currently effective laws.**

The federal government, many states, and commercial companies publish both print and digital versions of codified statutes.

- These versions are identical, and while the print version published by the federal or state government is usually the officially adopted version, this is not an important distinction, except for purposes of citation.
- Commercial versions of state and federal laws often include information that helps you better understand and apply the statute. For example, commercial versions of the United States Code (like the *United States Code Service* on Lexis and the *United States Code Annotated* on Westlaw) include, in addition to the text of all federal statutes, short descriptions of cases that interpret each section of the U.S. Code, information about the history of each section and its amendments, and references to related primary and secondary authorities.

Important pieces of legislation come to be known by their "popular names." When lawyers talk about a particular named law using its popular name, they are usually referring to the current version of the law, as amended and codified.

- Lawyers — especially those who specialize in a particular area of practice — often refer to statutes by their names when enacted (i.e., their popular names). So, civil rights lawyers will refer to the Voting Rights Act, labor lawyers to sections of the Americans with Disabilities Act, and securities attorneys to the Securities Act of 1933. When they do so, those lawyers are not, of course, referring to those laws as they were originally passed by Congress, but rather to the current versions of those laws, as amended over time and codified in the U.S. Code.

HOW IT WORKS: AN EXAMPLE

A mere six weeks after September 11, 2001, and as a reaction to the September 11 attacks, Congress passed the USA Patriot Act. The full name of the law passed by Congress is Uniting and Strengthening America by Providing Appropriate Tools Required to Intercept and Obstruct Terrorism Act of 2001; its designation is Public Law 107-56.

The bill that became the Patriot Act was introduced in Congress on October 23, 2001, and was enacted only three days later, with little debate or discussion. The Patriot Act's 130 pages address many different topics, including wire-tapping and other intelligence measures; criminal money-laundering; counterfeiting; visas, passports, and immigration; aid to victims of terrorism; and hazardous materials licenses. Many of the Patriot Act's provisions were immediately effective — activities that had *not* been prohibited prior to its passage suddenly were. The Patriot Act included entirely new provisions and also amended many existing laws.

What happened after the Patriot Act was passed? First, the government published the text of the Patriot Act as a Public Law (Public Law 107-56); next, it was incorporated into the *Statutes at Large* (its citation there is 115 Stat. 272 (2001)); and finally the Office of the Law Revision Counsel of the U.S. House of Representatives integrated the many provisions of the Patriot Act into the U.S. Code.

When the Patriot Act was codified, its provisions were scattered among fourteen of the fifty-four titles of the U.S. Code. So, for example, the wire-tapping and intelligence sections of the Patriot Act are codified in Title 18 of the U.S. Code (Crimes and Criminal Procedure); the criminal money laundering sections in Title 31 (Money and Finance); the visas and passports

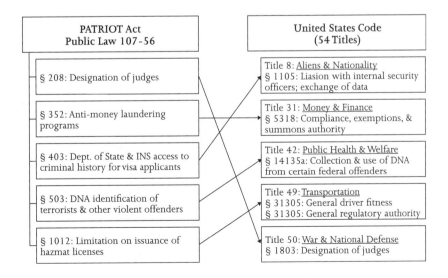

sections in Title 8 (Aliens and Nationality); the aid to victims of terrorism in Title 42 (Public Health and Welfare); and the provisions related to hazardous materials licenses in Title 49 (Transportation).

More than a decade and a half has gone by since Congress passed the Patriot Act. Many of the provisions originally included in the Patriot Act have themselves been amended by subsequent legislation. As Congress passes new legislation, the Office of Law Revision Counsel continues to update and revise the U.S. Code to reflect that new legislation.

WRITING ABOUT STATUTES

Understanding how to use statutes will help you decide if you have found what you need as you research. Here are some key points about working with and writing about statutes.

Connections: Appendix A tells you some of the many ways to find applicable statutes. You don't always have to start by searching a code. You may find references to statutes in secondary sources or in cases. Statutes will appear when you do a word search electronically, whether on a free or commercial service. Your careful reading and analysis of the component parts will help you discover if the statute applies to your case.

1. *Remember weight of authority principles*. Statutes are primary authority. If they are within your jurisdiction, they are binding. When your audience is legally trained, you won't need to mention that they are binding. You will, however, need that knowledge to inform your writing.

2. *If you find a statute and a case interpreting that statute, the statute outweighs the case*. Often you will organize your analysis to reflect this hierarchy, quoting the relevant parts of the statute before you write about the cases. You will usually start the discussion section of a memo or the argument section of a brief by setting out the statute, if one applies.

3. *Read every word*. If you are like most students, you may want to skip reading the statute, thinking that cases will tell you the important parts. This is a mistake! The ability to understand a statute through close reading is one of the most important skills to develop in law school. Don't let yourself off the hook. Read every word of applicable statutes every time.

4. *Break down the statute into its component parts*. You will need to discern exactly what the statute requires to know whether it applies and how it affects your case. Many lawyers use outlines or diagrams to understand statutes. There isn't just one way to break down the parts of the statute — it's more an art than a science. But it will help you know what may be at issue. Sometimes you may find a statute that seems like it should apply, but when you analyze the component parts, it does not.

5. *Notice whether the component parts are mandatory, prohibitory, or discretionary.* A mandatory rule tells you that someone "must" or "shall" do something. A prohibitory rule tells you that someone "must not" or "shall not" do something. A discretionary rule tells you that someone "may" do something.

6. *Match the statute's component parts with the facts of your legal problem.* This will let you focus on the parts of the statute that are at issue, and as you advance, it may help you research related sources or issues. The next chapter addresses these more complex questions.

7. *Most often you will organize your writing around the organization of the statute.* You will explain to your reader which parts of the statute will be contested, and you'll analyze each contested component separately — usually in the same order as the statute organized them.

8. *Choose precise subjects and verbs.* The wrong choice will mark you as a novice.

   Precise Subjects: The component parts of the statute may be *elements* or *factors*. These words are not synonymous or interchangeable. *Elements* are components of the statute that a party *must* prove; they are mandatory. If there are five elements, the plaintiff must prove all five. We use the word "meet" as a synonym with "prove" when writing about elements: i.e., "The plaintiff can meet the intent element." The word "and" often indicates elements. We say the statute is "written in the conjunctive" when we see the word "and." On the other hand, the word "or" means you may need to prove either of two things. We say the statute is "written in the disjunctive" when we see the word "or."

   Factors, on the other hand, are components the court will weigh, balance, or consider when deciding an issue. Factors often appear in a list, and decision-makers are most often asked to "consider" all of them. But the party need not *prove* all the factors. If there are five factors and a party can show some, it may be unnecessary to show the others. The court may balance two factors or interests, but courts do not "balance" or "weigh" the elements of a statute.

   Precise Verbs:

Statutes might . . .	Statutes don't . . .
"provide"	"say"
"require"	"hold"
"allow"	"find"
"prohibit"	"note"
"prescribe" (certain behaviors)	"argue"
"establish" (rights or duties)	"reason"

9. *Refer to the 'right' version of the statute.* While it's fine in conversation or sometimes even in oral advocacy to informally refer to a statute by its popular name, without more, when you communicate in writing there's an expectation that your references will be more formal and precise.

Consider this paragraph from the Supreme Court's decision in Shelby County v. Holder, 1333 S. Ct. 2612 (2013):

> Inspired to action by the civil rights movement, Congress responded in 1965 with the Voting Rights Act. Section 2 was enacted to forbid, in all 50 States, any "standard, practice, or procedure . . . imposed or applied . . . to deny or abridge the right of any citizen of the United States to vote on account of race or color." 79 Stat. 437. The current version forbids any "standard, practice, or procedure" that "results in a denial or abridgement of the right of any citizen of the United States to vote on account of race or color." 42 U.S.C. §1973(a).

In the first sentence, the Court refers to the Voting Rights Act as it was passed in 1965, and so, writes about the **Statutes at Large**. Remember that the **Statutes at Large** include all laws passed by Congress during a particular legislative session. In the first sentence the Court is discussing history and cites to a fundamental provision within the original Voting Rights Act passed by Congress back in 1965. By the second sentence the Court has moved on to the current text of that statute and, then, cites to the current United States Code. Cite to the source that actually contains the information you are discussing.

EXAMPLES AND EXPLANATIONS

Examples

Test yourself on the example questions below. Explain your answers to yourself, in your own words. Sometimes more than one answer may be correct. Then skip down to the explanations to check your answers.

1. You are researching an issue that falls under the provisions of a federal statute that was passed in 1998. You find a 2004 case from the United States Supreme Court interpreting a term in the statute. The statute was amended to clarify the same term in 2008.

Part A. You've broken the statute into component parts, mentally matching it with your facts, and it applies to your case. That means you'll use the statute. Will you also use the United States Supreme Court case?

(1) Yes, because the United States Supreme Court is the highest court in the land.

(2) Yes, if the Public Law Number was unchanged.

(3) No, because what the statute says outweighs the case.

(4) No, if after reading the amendment and the case you are satisfied that the amendment changes the meaning of the term the case had interpreted.

Part B. How should you organize your analysis of the issue governed by the statute?

(1) You should start by setting out the statute.

(2) You should organize the entire analysis using the same organization of the component parts that the statute uses.

(3) You should start with the cases interpreting the statute because they explain what the statute means.

(4) You should begin by telling the history of the statute and how Congress amended it.

2. You are researching a federal issue relating to the Voting Rights Act, and find the session law, the official codified law, and the commercial version of the codified law. Which of the following statements are true?

(1) The three are interchangeable because the text of the law is the same in all three.

(2) Although the text is the same, the three are not interchangeable because court rules require you to cite to the official codified version.

(3) The session law is the most important because it includes the text actually passed by the legislature.

(4) Reading the commercial version either online or in print will lead me to other related sources.

3. Your supervising attorney has asked you to find "the Civil Rights Act of 1964." Which of the following statements are true?

(1) You should do historical research into the Act because the Civil Rights Movement was a long time ago and lawyers wouldn't ask for the "1964 Act" unless they wanted those old statutes.

(2) It's always a good idea to look for references to regulations that implement the statute and cases that interpret the statute.

(3) The statute is old, so the best authority will be the many cases interpreting it. You can skip finding or reading the actual statute. The cases are more important here because of the age of the statute.

(4) You should not start with historical research because most lawyers want to know the law as it exists today.

4. Here is part of the federal statute governing failure to pay legal child support obligations:

    (a) Offense. — Any person who —

    (1) willfully fails to pay a support obligation with respect to a child who resides in another State, if such obligation has remained unpaid for a period longer than 1 year, or is greater than $5,000;

    (2) travels in interstate or foreign commerce with the intent to evade a support obligation, if such obligation has remained unpaid for a period longer than 1 year, or is greater than $5,000; or

    (3) willfully fails to pay a support obligation with respect to a child who resides in another State, if such obligation has remained unpaid for a period longer than 2 years, or is greater than $10,000;

    shall be punished as provided in subsection (c).

    List the problems with these sentences about the statute:

    The federal statute governing failure to pay legal child support obligations, 18 U.S.C. §228, holds that the government must prove all three factors. The first element notes that the support obligation must be in excess of $5000 or have remained unpaid for more than 1 year. Another factor the court considers is whether the accused has traveled overseas. Finally, the last provision argues the government can press this statute even if the deadbeat dad is just in another state for 2 years.

5. Remember the smartphone-controlled paper airplane and the potential for raising funds by selling company stock on a crowdfunding site? The legislation that authorized this kind of financing was part of the Jumpstart Our Business Startups Act (the JOBS Act) passed by Congress during the 112th legislative session.

    - The bill number of the JOBS Act was H.R. 3606;
    - Its public law number is 112-106;
    - Its citation in the *Statutes at Large* is 126 Stat. 306 (2012);
    - The crowdfunding provisions of the JOBS Act are in sections 301-304 of the public law; and
    - Those sections of the JOBS Act are codified in Title 15 of the U.S. Code, sections 77d, 77d-1, 77r, 78c, 78l, and 78o.

    If you represent the entrepreneur who wants to develop the smartphone-controlled paper airplane and you want to investigate whether she might sell shares in her company on a crowdfunding site, what source would you first look to?

    (1) the original Public Law
    (2) the Statutes at Large
    (3) the U.S. Code

Explanations

1. Part A: (1) Incorrect. Even though the United States Supreme Court is the highest court in the federal system, the Court is bound by the new text of the amendment. Even the Court itself would say the 2004 case was "superseded" by the amendment. (2) Incorrect. The Public Law Number is just the number given to the bill as it becomes law and before it is arranged topically in the code as a statute. This answer doesn't make sense. (3) Correct. But a poor choice of verb! Statutes don't "say." You could write: No, because the statute outweighs the case. (4) Correct. You would want to read the statute, the case, and the amendment to really understand if the case has become useless. Parts of the case may still be good law, and you would want to analyze exactly how the amendment changes things.

1. Part B: (1) Correct. The beginning of your analysis may include additional components, such as a thesis statement, but somewhere at or near the beginning you will set out the statute. (2) Correct. When you break the statute into its component parts, you'll use that same organization to write your analysis. (3) Incorrect. You should start with the statute, quoting the exact text. You'll then add the cases that interpret the statute. (4) Incorrect. Most legal readers don't want to take the time to read the history of the statute unless the nature of the history is an issue in your analysis. Your readers will probably be happiest if you just start by quoting the relevant parts of the statute.

2. (1) Incorrect. Remember that extraneous, non-binding parts of the session laws are often deleted when they are codified. Examples of the kind of text deleted are the preambles, or references within the session law to itself. (2) Correct. Courts have often adopted rules that require lawyers to cite to the official version of a statute. The text of the statute is the same in the official version as it is in the commercially published version. Commercially published codes usually include a citation to the official version of the statute. It is fine to rely on the commercially published code and to cite to the official version. (3) Incorrect. While the session law is the text that was passed by the legislature, that distinction is usually unimportant once the session law is codified. As legislatures pass laws that amend other laws, they are amending the codified version of the statute and not the session law. (4) Correct. Commercial versions of statutes usually include abstracts of cases that have applied the statute, citations to other primary authorities that relate to your statute, references to secondary sources that discuss the statute, and the history of the statute.

3. (1) Probably incorrect. Unless your supervisor has specifically asked you to research the history, you would research the statute as it is today. Then you'll read closely to analyze which parts of the statute will be at issue, and then you'll look for the best authority addressing those issues. (2) Correct. Always be aware that you may need to find regulations

interpreting the statute. (3) Incorrect. The statute is the controlling authority. The text of the statute governs. The cases interpreting it are important, but close reading of the statute is always the key when you have a governing statute. (4) Correct.

4. Here is a list. See if you found these and perhaps more.

   1. Statutes don't "hold."

   2. Moreover, this statute does *not* require that the government prove that the individual engaged in all three of the activities (and if it did, those three activities would be "elements," not "factors"). Rather, if the government can prove any one of (1), (2), or (3), the individual will be subject to punishment.

   3. Statutes don't typically "note."

   4. "Another factor the court considers . . ." The three activities enumerated in the statute are neither elements nor factors. If it proves that any one of the three activities occurred, the government will have satisfied the statute and the individual will be subject to punishment.

   5. The phrase "has traveled overseas" is problematic. The statute's precise language matters. Most often you will quote it. You would most probably write about "travels in interstate or foreign commerce with the intent to evade a support obligation . . ."

   6. Provisions and statutes don't "argue."

   7. The author of the passage failed to note the "or" at the end of (2). That "or" means the statute is written in the disjunctive. The prosecution can show either (1) or (2) or (3).

   8. "Press this statute" probably derives from "pressing charges," but it would be more professional to write that the government can or cannot successfully prosecute.

5. (1) and (2) Incorrect. The JOBS Act was passed in 2013. If you look at the JOBS Act as a public law or at its version in the Statutes at Large, you risk relying on statutory language that may have been changed in subsequent sessions of Congress. Moreover, you would not be able to see the crowdfunding provisions in the context of related laws. If you wanted to learn about the history of the crowdfunding provisions and understand what policies Congress sought to further in enacting the JOBS Act, you might look at the public law or the Statutes at Large version. But you certainly wouldn't start your research in those sources. (3) Correct. The U.S. Code would be your first source to research, as it contains all of the current and enforceable federal legislation and includes all amendments and other revisions to federal statutes. Looking at the crowdfunding provisions in the U.S. Code means that you are seeing the *current* law on crowdfunding and you are seeing it in relation to other statutory provisions that may affect its interpretation.

Legislation In Action

When you first read a statute, it's almost like visiting a foreign country and trying to understand what's being said. The language used in statutes is stilted and formal—there are lots of clauses joined in inexplicable and complicated ways, and there are new additions to your vocabulary at every turn. The first chapter on legislation introduced you to the basics—how statutes come into being, how they are codified, and how you write about them. This chapter goes one step further; it will help you read and understand statutes, relate them to other legislation, and appreciate and work with the organization of sections within a statutory code. We'll work through three examples, going from the simple to the complex, approaching the research problem as a practicing attorney might. In each case, we'll see that, in any research in statutes, you'll need to both understand the big picture—what the statute seeks to accomplish and how it relates to other statutes—and dive into the weeds of the statute's text, investigating what the words used actually mean and how the clauses of a particular section work together.

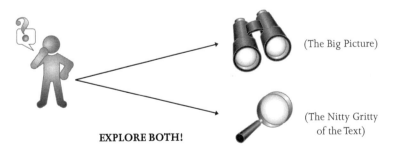

(The Big Picture)

(The Nitty Gritty of the Text)

EXPLORE BOTH!

Before we get to our sample problems, we'll need to cover some first steps in beginning research in any area you think might be governed by statutes.

THE PRELIMINARIES

You should begin just about any research task by thinking about whether a federal or state statute (or both!) might apply.

- Statutes govern all sorts of activities and behaviors. For example, criminal statutes set forth the elements of crimes; environmental statutes tell us what we can and cannot do with natural resources; labor legislation describes the relationships and rights among employers and employees; and intellectual property statutes establish ownership rights for authors and artists.

- If there's one area where we can be sure that statutes apply, it's the economy. Whether it's banking, taxes, bankruptcy, or finance, there is sure to be some overarching legislative scheme that determines how things work and what activities can and cannot be undertaken. We need statutes to provide this structure and to give the necessary authority to the executive branches of state and federal governments and their administrative agencies. Because case law addresses specific disputes among individual parties, we don't expect case law to organize an area of commerce — or, in fact, any activity — and dictate the kinds of behaviors that are permitted within it.

- As you gain experience, you'll develop a sense of whether federal or state statutes — or both — will apply to your research task. As a novice researcher, begin by figuring out whether a federal statute applies. If it's a topic governed by federal law — like health care, the environment, or immigration — federal statutes will be important. But check state statutes as well. Many questions involve both state and federal statutes. You need to be thorough and identify all statutes that might apply.

- If you're trying to structure a transaction so that your client will realize certain benefits that are conferred by state or federal governments (e.g., tax benefits), statutes will govern. Similarly, if your client needs licenses, permits, or other kinds of permission to engage in particular types of activities (e.g., construction, mining, or nursing), your research will focus initially on state and federal statutes and their application.

Connections: If you think that both federal and state statutes might apply, research federal legislation first. You might find that the federal legislation pre-empts state action on your topic. Even when that's not the case, state statutes sometimes refer to federal legislation and are drafted in the context of the federal statutory scheme. An example:

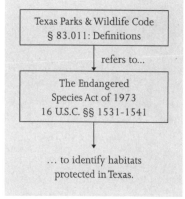

Texas Parks & Wildlife Code § 83.011: Definitions

refers to...

The Endangered Species Act of 1973 16 U.S.C. §§ 1531-1541

... to identify habitats protected in Texas.

Get a broad — but not necessarily deep — understanding of the statutory scheme from a secondary source.

- As a beginner, you may not know much at all about the way in which the federal government or the states manage and govern an area of commerce or other activity. You probably don't know the lingo that experts employ. To begin to understand the area of law and its important terms and to identify the statutes that govern, use an introductory secondary source — whether it's a reliable and current website you find by using Google or a treatise or legal encyclopedia available to you in print or in a legal research database.

Where you want to go determines how you get there. Adapt your research to the kind of question you've been asked to answer.

- Your research goal may be very specific; for example, you might be asked to find the definition of arson in Texas. Or, your research question may be much broader; for example, what rights will I gain and what rights will I give up if my fellow employees vote to enter into a collective bargaining agreement? In answering a very specific question, it may be easiest to simply do a word search within a specific title or chapter of a statutory code (in our arson example, the Texas criminal or penal code) to find the answer. But as the research question expands, you will probably be better off looking at the relevant statute as a whole and figuring out the relationships among its different sections. You wouldn't want to rely on a single section of a code and not realize that other sections may qualify that section, expand upon it, provide exemptions from it, or define the terms used in it.

Now let's work through three tasks that involve researching and understanding statutes.

TASK 1: WHAT'S THE CALIFORNIA STATUTE OF LIMITATIONS FOR BURGLARY?

Don't expect that even the most straightforward of research assignments will be answered by a single section of a statutory code. To find laws about crimes in California you would look to the California Penal Code. There are six parts of that Penal Code, but only two of them look like they would be helpful in answering the statute of limitations question. Part 1 ("Of Crimes and Punishments") of the Penal Code describes the elements of crimes in California and the punishments for those crimes, and Part 2 ("Of Criminal Procedure") outlines the process by which crimes are prosecuted. So, Part 1 deals with the **substance** of crimes and punishments and Part 2 with the **process** by which criminal prosecutions take place.

Statutes of limitations relate to the process of criminal prosecution, rather than to the substance of crimes, so you should search the criminal procedure part of the California Penal Code for laws that provide time limits for prosecuting crimes. Chapter 2 within the criminal procedure part of the Penal Code is titled "Time of Commencing Criminal Actions." There isn't a section within that Chapter that specifically applies to burglary. By looking at the table of contents for the time limits chapter, you'll see that the time limits within which a crime must be prosecuted depend on the potential punishment for the crime.

§ 800: Offenses Punishable by Imprisonment for Eight Years or More

§ 801: Offenses Punishable by Imprisonment

To determine the statute of limitations for burglary, we'll need to find the punishment for the crime of burglary. The definitions of crimes and the punishments for those crimes are set forth in Part 1 of the California Penal Code (i.e., the "substance" part of the Penal Code). It's easy enough to simply search for "burglary" within Part 1 and quickly find these two sections in the chapter titled "Burglary":

§ 459: Definition

§ 461: Punishment

Section 461 provides that the crime of burglary may be punished by imprisonment for anywhere from one to six years. Knowing that, we can go back to § 801 of the procedure part of the Penal Code. Section 801 requires that prosecutions of burglary commence within three years after the offense was committed.

Here's how the sections of the Penal Code fit together to answer our relatively simple question:

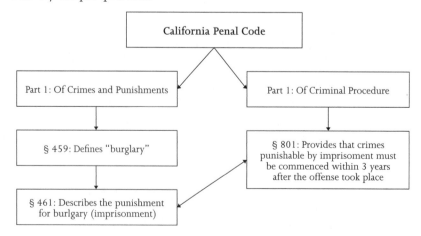

TASK 2: CAN MY EMPLOYER ENFORCE MANDATORY RETIREMENT AT A CERTAIN AGE?

This question is more complex. For one thing, we don't know whether federal or state statutes — or both — might apply. Begin your research by looking at the U.S. Code. The title that is likely to be most helpful is Title 29 (Labor). The table of contents for a chapter or title of a statutory code is a good place to start if you want to get a sense of how the different sections of a chapter or title fit together. For our mandatory retirement example, we would look to the table of contents of Chapter 14 of Title 29 (Labor) of the U.S. Code. Chapter 14 is titled "Age Discrimination in Employment" and includes §§ 621 through 634.

Chapter 14: Age Discrimination in Employment

621. Congressional statement of findings and purpose — **POLICIES AND PURPOSES**

622. Education and research program; recommendation to Congress

623. Prohibition of age discrimination — **THE GENERAL RULE**

624. Study by Secretary of Labor; reports to President and Congress; scope of study; implementation of study; transmittal date of reports

625. Administration

626. Recordkeeping, investigation, and enforcement — **COMPLIANCE AND ENFORCEMENT**

627. Notices to be posted

628. Rules and regulations; exemptions — **POSSIBLE EXCEPTIONS TO THE RULE**

629. Criminal penalties — **WHAT HAPPENS IF YOU DON'T COMPLY**

630. Definitions — **WHAT THE TERMS USED IN THE STATUTE MEAN**

631. Age limits — **MORE IINFORMATION ON THE RULE**

633. Federal-State relationship — **CAN STATES ACT?**

633a. Nondiscrimination on account of age in Federal Government employment

634. Authorization of appropriations

Section 623 gives us the general rule — it is unlawful for an employer to fire or to refuse to hire an individual or otherwise discriminate against the individual because of his or her age. The table of contents allows us to identify other relevant sections that expand upon the general rule. We see the potential for exceptions (§ 628), the consequences of non-compliance (§ 629), and guidance on how to comply (§ 626).

Having identified the relevant parts of the U.S. Code, you'll need to read the statutes carefully. Statutes are not easy to read, but there's no substitute for reading them. Even the best secondary source can only describe a statute. When you write about statutes, you must refer to the text of the statute itself and not to its description in a secondary source. To be able to write sensibly about a statute, you will need to have spent time working through its text to understand its structure and organization and the meaning of the terms used in it.

This doesn't mean that you have to read sections that are not relevant to your research. In this example, it's easy to see that there are sections of the chapter on age discrimination that you can skim or even ignore altogether. We don't really care about the recommendations or the study or reports referenced in §§ 622 and 624 and, since your client is not the federal government, § 633a is inapplicable as well. Our concern is not the funding of government enforcement, so § 634 is off the table too. To answer the client's question, we'll need to focus on the rule established by the statute (§ 623), exceptions to that rule (§628), the meanings of the terms used in the statute (§ 630), means of compliance (§ 626), and consequences of non-compliance (§ 629).

As you read the relevant sections, look closely at the structure and language of each section. The general rule prohibiting age discrimination in employment is set forth in § 623.

---

29 U.S.C. § 623: Prohibition of age discrimination.

(a) It shall be unlawful for an employer –

1) to fail or refuse to hire or to discharge any individual or otherwise discriminate against any individual with respect to his compensation, terms, conditions, or privileges of employment, because of such individual's age;

2) to limit, segregate, or classify his employees in any way which would deprive or tend to deprive any individual of employment opportunities or otherwise adversely affect his status as an employee, because of such individual's age; **or**

3) to reduce the wage rate of any employee in order to comply with this chapter.

Recognize that when clauses are joined by an "and," *each* of the conditions set forth in those clauses must be satisfied in order for the rule to apply. If the clauses are joined by an "or," any one of them will suffice to trigger the application of the rule. If an employer does any one of the actions described in any part of paragraph (a) of § 623, the employer will have violated the statute.

As this example illustrates, statutes often set forth a rule, exceptions to the rule, means of compliance, and penalties for non-compliance. The terms used in the rule are often defined, either in the statute itself or by reference to other sections in the code. Expect to see those different provisions when you read a statute. **Don't stop reading after you've found the rule.** Sometimes the definitions precede the section that sets forth the rule; sometimes (as in this case) the definitions follow. And sometimes the definitions are included in the section that contains the rule itself.

And, finally, as you read the statute, keep in mind the policies that it was designed to further. Some statutes very explicitly describe the reasons for their enactment. Section 621 ("Congressional Statements of Findings and Purpose") tells us what Congress hoped to accomplish and gives us some context to help us understand the substantive provisions. Reading a statute in light of what it was intended to do will help you make sense of its provisions.

Once you've finished researching federal statutes, you'll need to check to see if state statutes might apply as well.

TASK 3: CAN I SELL STOCK IN MY COMPANY ON A CROWDFUNDING SITE?

Remember the smartphone-controlled paper airplane from Chapter 3? Suppose your client is the developer of that technology. Let's call her Enid. She has a great idea for a smartphone app, but lacks the funds to develop the technology, market the product, and then get it to consumers. Fortunately, Enid has lots of friends who are willing to invest in her project (and who all want to share in the monetary rewards that her success will bring!). As Enid's lawyer, you've already helped her form a corporation in the jurisdiction in which she resides. She'll use that corporation as the vehicle for developing and selling her app.

Enid now comes to you and says, "I want to sell stock in my company on a crowdfunding site like SeedInvest or Kickstarter. How do I do that?"

This is a hard question to answer. Enid is not asking you what the consequences of a particular action would be or whether certain activities are prohibited. Instead, she is planning for the future and trying to find a mechanism that will bring capital into her corporation and allow her to produce and market her product. She hopes that crowdfunding might provide a means to do so. Your job is to figure out whether crowdfunding makes sense for Enid and her corporation and, if it does, to structure a transaction so that Enid realizes the benefits she is expecting (and more!).

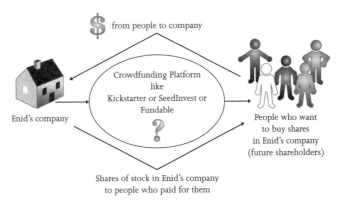

Remember that statutes may not only prohibit activity; they may also dictate how to obtain certain benefits or privileges. Many statutes are discretionary, which means that there is no absolute requirement that persons comply with the statute. But there might be benefits available to them if they do comply. These discretionary statutes often read like a road map, providing information about the steps that must be taken in order to qualify for a benefit or avoid a penalty. Compliance with those statutes gives clients some certainty as to the consequences of their actions.

Google is not a bad place to begin your research. You can quickly get a sense of what crowdfunding is and, with a little digging, at least an appreciation of the issues associated with the sale of shares of a company's stock through a crowdfunding platform. Once you have a very basic understanding, turn to a reliable secondary source. Some secondary sources, like hornbooks, are geared specifically toward students and are intended to help students master a particular course topic. Other secondary sources, like legal encyclopedias and ALRs, are intended for the general practitioner. Still other sources, like multi-volume treatises, are designed to serve practitioners in a particular area. Use the secondary source that best serves your purpose. In many contexts, a multi-volume treatise (either in print or in legal research databases) written for practicing lawyers in a particular area will be most useful in helping you understand the intricacies of a statutory scheme. Chapter 10 describes secondary sources more thoroughly and will help you get a sense of which secondary source might be most helpful in different circumstances.

After consulting secondary sources, you learn that any sale of shares of stock in a company has the potential for triggering the registration requirements of the federal securities laws [specifically, the Securities Act of 1933, which is codified in Chapter 2A ("Securities and Trust Indentures") of Title 15 (Commerce and Trade) of the U.S. Code]. At some point in your research, you'll be ready to look at the statutes themselves, and you'll find that there are many sections within Chapter 2A. Do not be alarmed. If your purpose is to figure out whether Enid can sell shares in her company on a crowdfunding platform and how she should go about doing so, there are many sections that you can quickly eliminate as not relevant. Sections that relate to enforcement and penalties, litigation, and procedure can all be bypassed for now. You may want to investigate those more closely later. Right now, you just need to tell Enid whether selling shares in her company on a crowdfunding platform is a possibility and describe what that might entail.

Once you've eliminated sections that appear not to be relevant to Enid's question, you're left with a relatively small number of sections that you will need to read closely.

Chapter 2A ("Securities and Trust Indentures") of Title 15 (Commerce and Trade) of the U.S. Code

§ 77b   Definitions; Promotion of Efficiency, Competition, and Capital Formation — DEFINITIONS

§ 77c   Classes of Securities Under this Subchapter

§ 77d   Exempted Transactions — EXCEPTIONS TO THE GENERAL RULE

§ 77d–1   Requirements with Respect to Certain Small Transactions

§ 77e   Prohibitions Relating to Interstate Commerce and the Mails — GENERAL RULE – NO SALES WITHOUT REGISTRATION

§ 77f   Registration of Securities

§ 77g   Information Required in Registration Statement

Connections: Experienced attorneys (including professors) sometimes talk about statutes by referring to their popular names. A securities attorney will refer to § 5 of the Securities Act of 1933 and a tax attorney will reference § 210 of the Internal Revenue Code.

Sometime it's easy — and intuitive — to make the transition from popular names to sections in the U.S. Code.

| § 210 of the Internal Revenue Code | = | 26 U.S.C. § 210 |

[The Internal Revenue Code **is** Title 26 of the U.S. Code and all section numbers correspond.]

Sometimes it's not so easy.

| § 5 of the Securities Act of 1933 | = | 17 U.S.C. § 77e |

All of the Securities Act of 1933 is codified in §§ 77a through 77xx of Title 17 (Commerce), "e" is the fifth letter of the alphabet and, so, § 5 of the Securities Act of 1933 corresponds to § 77e in Title 17. How would you know this? Secondary sources almost provide the official citation to codified statute. Or, you could simply Google the popular name and section number; it's likely that many results will set forth the U.S.C. citation.

Here, the general rule — that companies may not sell securities (i.e., shares of their stock) in public transactions without first registering the stock with the Securities and Exchange Commission ("SEC") — is set forth in § 77e. You can quickly glean by a few Internet searches that registration of securities with the SEC — this is what happens when companies "go public" — is a very expensive proposition (in the range of hundreds of thousands to millions of dollars) and one that Enid cannot afford. At this point you know that you can probably get by without reading §§ 77f and 77g, since both of those relate to the registration of securities (and Enid wants to avoid that at all costs).

Your next avenue to explore is the availability of an exemption from the registration requirement. Fortunately, the exemption section is well-titled. Section 77d ("Exempted Transactions") lists several types of transactions that can qualify for an exemption from the registration requirements of the Securities Act. If Enid's company sells its shares of stock in a transaction that is described in §77d as being exempt, her company will not have to register the shares with the SEC. Section 77d lists seven exemptions, most of which are only available if the company selling its shares meets certain conditions and sells its stock in a particular way. Of those seven exemptions, only four are available to a company selling its own shares. Now you will need to read those four paragraphs within § 77d very carefully. And, as you read those paragraphs, you'll want to refer back to § 77b to see what and how terms are defined.

By looking at the organization of the Securities Act and its constituent parts, by checking with secondary sources from time to time, and by process of elimination, we've been able to whittle down the pool of relevant sections to just one, and within that one section, to four paragraphs. Unfortunately, nowhere in those four paragraphs — or anywhere in § 77d — will you find any reference to crowdfunding. What that means for you and Enid is that you will need to structure a transaction that satisfies the conditions set forth in one of those four paragraphs if Enid's company is to sell shares of its stock without registering them. If you can find a way to do that on a crowdfunding platform, her crowdfunding idea just might work.

What you'll find as you read these paragraphs is that they're not particularly specific. Because the risks associated with not qualifying for an exemption are so high (ever heard of securities fraud?), Enid needs certainty about whether her company's sales of stock qualify for an exemption. In securities, as is the case in most areas of the law that deal with the economy and finance, administrative regulations become all important. The statute may set forth a very general rule, but Congress leaves it to the appropriate administrative agency to formulate more precise directives and instructions for compliance. The next step in your research would be to turn to a sophisticated secondary source and then to the SEC regulations themselves. We'll save that for another chapter.

EXAMPLES AND EXPLANATIONS

Examples

It's always good to get some hands-on experience. Here are some questions that will allow you to practice researching statutes. Law is open-ended, changing as time passes. And the tools to find law are open-ended, changing often just like the law. Thus, the questions below are open-ended so that you can strike out on your own path without needing to replicate someone else's out-of-date research. Take our questions as a starting point and see where you go. The Explanations discuss some of the things you may see on your research path. Remember that if you need help learning how to use various tools to search, look to Appendix A.

1. "Adverse Possession" is a way one can acquire title to real property by fulfilling certain conditions. It is a way to put ownership in the hands of those who put land to use. Most jurisdictions have at least some statutory requirements for adverse possession. Find the adverse possession statute for your state. If you cannot find the statute in your state, find the statute for a neighboring one. What must a plaintiff prove to establish ownership through adverse possession?

2. You plan to make a policy argument in an office memorandum discussing a fair housing discrimination claim. You are deciding whether to bring the case to a state or federal court. Look for both state and federal housing discrimination statutes. Is there anything in the statutes that will help you support a policy argument?

3. How is the sentencing scheme different for robbery and armed robbery in your state? Is it the same in a neighboring state?
4. Find and compare which employers fall under the federal age discrimination statute and the federal disability discrimination statute.

Explanations

1. Adverse Possession

Most states will require that possession be:

- actual
- hostile or non-permissive
- open and notorious
- continuous; and
- exclusive

Some states will require that possession be:

- under claim of title or claim of right (occupier believes he or she holds title)
- under color of title (possessing a deed that incorrectly gives occupier title)
- payment of property taxes

2. Fair Housing Policy

Connections: Sometimes you'll find that the statute only sets out some of these requirements, but cases establish more requirements. For research to be complete, you'll need to find those expansions on the rule. You will also find that cases illustrate how courts understand the various requirements — so cases may tell you what it means to be "continuous" or "hostile."

You probably had no problem using either a free online search or a commercial service to find the federal Fair Housing Act. At the beginning of 42 U.S.C. § 3601, you will find the "Declaration of Policy," which states: "It is the policy of the United States to provide, within constitutional limitations, for fair housing throughout the United States."

For fair housing law in the states, a simple Google search gave us several websites that list state and local fair housing enforcement laws. To use commercial services you would choose a specific state to explore, because choosing a database that gives you results for all fifty states would likely be too bulky. Once you find the statute, whether federal or state, remember that policy statements are most often included near the beginning of the statute. If you find nothing useful within the statute itself, you would turn to other authorities.

Connections: If you don't find policy statements within the statute itself, you can turn to other primary authorities — either cases or regulations — to look for policy statements. Cases interpreting a fair housing statute likely will include policy statements from the courts.

Regulations, always related to statutes, may also include policy statements. For example, here is language from California where regulation 2 CCR § 11006 explains the policy in the California fair housing act:

> The public policy of the State of California is to protect and safeguard the civil rights of all individuals to seek, have access to, obtain, and hold employment without discrimination because of race, religious creed, color, national origin, ancestry, physical disability, mental disability, medical condition, genetic information, marital status, sex, gender, gender identity, gender expression, age for individuals over forty years of age, and sexual orientation. Employment practices should treat all individuals equally, evaluating each on the basis of individual skills, knowledge and abilities and not on the basis of characteristics generally attributed to a group enumerated in the Act. The objectives of the California Fair Employment and Housing Act and these regulations are to promote equal employment opportunity and to assist all persons in understanding their rights, duties and obligations, so as to facilitate achievement of voluntary compliance with the law.

One of the joys of using commercial research services is that they are likely to give you search results that provide the connections you need. For example, all of the commercial services are going to offer you cases, regulations, and secondary sources that relate to your statute. If you are using free sources, remember that you may need to do several searches to find the same connecting sources.

3. **Robbery Sentencing**

If you looked at more than one state, you may have seen that the terminology states use in sentencing those convicted of robbery vary widely. Some states differentiate "degrees" or "classes" of crimes or felonies. Generally speaking and all other things being equal, robbery with a weapon will always result in a longer sentence than robbery without a weapon. Perhaps you found distinctions based on whether an accomplice was present, whether someone uninvolved in the crime was injured, or whether the convicted defendant has a record of previous convictions. Other states may find different factors to enhance or extend a sentence based on the age of the victim, or whether the act was committed in a school or a place of worship. Sometimes enhancements may apply to more than one crime, and you will find the enhancements elsewhere in the criminal code, not simply by finding the robbery statute.

4. **Employers under Federal Age and Disability Discrimination Statutes**

Probably the first thing you needed to do as you researched this question was to make sure you understood the different acronyms that identify various federal discrimination statutes. Usually this is easily and cheaply accomplished by a free search. Several websites list the statutes by topic, the acronym they are known by, and their official names. Appendix A suggests that you think about the credibility and reliability of the various free resources. The connection between statutes and administrative law is evident again because a government agency, the Equal Employment Opportunity Commission (EEOC), offers websites detailing information for various statutes. These sites are reliable and easily available.

You'll learn that the federal Age Discrimination in Employment Act of 1967 is commonly known as the ADEA. Title I and Title V of the Americans with Disabilities Act of 1990 as amended constitute the ADA. Another federal statute, the Rehabilitation Act of 1973, prohibits discrimination against disabled individuals who work in the federal government. Once you are secure that you know what you are looking for, your search can go to the requirements of the individual statutes. The information you seek is most likely on the same general websites you found in your initial search. Or you might find a good summary in the secondary sources you found in a search on a commercial service. But you will need better authority than citing to secondary sources, whether from a commercial service or a summary on a website. You'll need to cite to primary authority — the statute itself. As always, there are lots of avenues to find the statute.

Once you've found the statutes, through either free or commercial searches, the next puzzle is finding the information you need about the businesses the statute applies to — who qualifies as an employer. Sometimes statutes are long and complex, and sometimes finding the precise information you need means reading much of it. But if you turn first to the statutory scheme at the beginning, you may find helpful shortcuts. If you looked there, and saw a definition section, you found a good shortcut. Information about those to whom the statute applies will often be there.

Identifying, Reading, Understanding, and Writing About Judicial Opinions

Your neighbor annoys you. A fan of both technology and snooping, Bart has taken to flying unmanned aerial vehicles over and into your back yard and all of his neighbors' yards as well. Bart's aerial intrusions have grown to be quite irritating. The buzzing drones are a nuisance and you feel like Bart is invading your personal space.

Nuisance and trespass are two torts traditionally governed by the common law. Disputes between neighbors over things like cutting down trees, shining bright lights in the night, and applying pesticides that drift onto adjacent property are the kinds of torts that trial and appellate courts have long considered. It is an easy enough task to use either keyword searching or a topical index — like Westlaw's Key Number System — to find cases that describe the kinds of activities that constitute a common law trespass to real property or a nuisance. It's pretty unlikely, though, that you will find many — or even any — cases that discuss drones in the context of their potential for trespasses and nuisance. Drone technology — at least in the hands of amateurs like Bart — is fairly new, and you would be a very lucky researcher indeed to find cases in your jurisdiction that deal with trespasses to real property or nuisances caused by drones. These neighborly disputes are unlikely to come to trial and even less likely to be appealed.

You need a strategy to help you find cases so you can determine whether Bart's activities might constitute either a trespass or a nuisance. Where would you start, and what are the best cases for helping you make a persuasive argument that Bart is trespassing or causing a nuisance? How would you weigh a case from another jurisdiction that applies nuisance doctrine to drones compared to a nuisance case from your own jurisdiction that involves a very different set of facts?

This chapter will introduce you to the basics of understanding cases. The chapter that follows sets out some examples that demonstrate how an attorney might find, evaluate, choose, and use cases in practice.

GLOSSARY

Common law: Judicial opinions that make law on a topic where there is no statutory or Constitutional authority.

Case law: Any judicial opinion, including the common law and cases interpreting statutes or Constitutional provisions.

Stare decisis: The principle that courts are bound by their own previous opinions as well as being bound by opinions from higher courts.

Concurrence: Opinion of a judge or judges who agree on the outcome of the case, but not the majority's rationale. (Concurrences are persuasive authority, not mandatory.)

Dissent: Opinion of a judge or judges who disagree with the majority's outcome and the rationale. (Dissents are persuasive authority, not mandatory.)

Plurality: Opinion from a group of judges where no single opinion received the support of the majority of judges.

En banc: When a case is heard by all the judges of a particular court sitting together, rather than a smaller panel.

Reporter: A book where cases are published chronologically, usually organized by jurisdiction.

Digest: A topical index to the issues in published opinions most often used when electronic resources for searching for cases are not available.

Dicta: Text in a court's opinion that is not essential to the holding of the case, and therefore is not the law.

Analogical argument: Arguments made by comparing the facts or policy in precedent cases to the facts or policy in your case.

Policy argument: Arguments that the court should decide a case in a particular way because the outcome would benefit society.

Common Law vs. Case Law

The United States, like most countries that were at one time British colonies, operates as a **common law** system. The "common law" is the law embodied in court opinions when the court is settling a dispute without the guidance of a statute. In common law systems, the court is bound by previous decisions within its jurisdiction under the principle of *stare decisis*.

The term **case law** refers to all cases the court decides, regardless of whether the opinion makes law or whether the court is interpreting a statute or determining how a statute applies to a particular set of facts. Thus, **case law** and **common law** are not synonyms. Case law includes common law, but the reverse is not true.

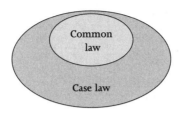

Because classes during the first year of law school are traditionally common law subjects, students often get the notion that most rules are found in cases. Remember that statutes also contain rules, and that when the court is interpreting a statute, it is bound by the text of the statute unless the statute is unconstitutional.

YOU NEED TO KNOW HOW IT'S MADE TO UNDERSTAND WHAT YOU ARE SEEING

Opinions that create binding law are the product of appellate courts. Although some trial courts issue opinions, those opinions are rarely mandatory authority for other courts. (See Chapter 2 for more on the intricate relationships among courts and jurisdictions that determine when one opinion is more important than another.)

In appellate courts, most often a panel of three to nine judges decides cases. Using the record of proceedings below, the briefs submitted by the parties, and sometimes after hearing oral argument, judges discuss the case and come to a preliminary decision. The chief judge of the court decides who will write the opinion.

The judge authoring the opinion will attempt to fashion a document that comports with each judge's reasons for reaching the outcome. If successful, a majority of judges will "sign" the opinion, and the "majority opinion" becomes the law. Sometimes cases are difficult to understand because there was disagreement on the panel, and the author needed to write an opinion that incorporates the reactions of several disparate factions on the court in order to garner enough signatures for a majority.

As the draft opinion is circulated within the court, each judge can choose to respond in several different ways. The judge can sign the opinion and be a part of the "majority." Alternatively, the judge can write a **concurrence**, a separate opinion that agrees with the outcome but for different reasons. Or the judge can disagree with the outcome and write a "dissent," a separate opinion that states why the judge disagrees with the reasoning and the outcome. Occasionally, ethical considerations will prompt a judge to abstain from the case completely. Only majority opinions are considered "the law." Concurrences and dissents may be persuasive authority, but they do not carry the force of law that majority opinions do, and other courts are not bound by them.

Rather than writing their own concurrences or dissents, judges may also decide to sign on to another judge's concurrence or dissent. When no one opinion garners enough votes for a majority, the court may issue a **plurality** opinion. Special rules apply when you are trying to state the "holding" in a plurality opinion; primarily, these require you to state the holding as a narrow rule that reflects the rationale of the largest number of judges.

The appellate courts in many jurisdictions hear cases in panels comprising a smaller number of judges than the entire court. When more of the jurisdiction's judges than usual hear the case sitting together, it is called **en banc**. Often hearing a case *en banc* means all the judges of a jurisdiction decide the case. The United States Supreme Court, for example, hears all cases "en banc." Other courts hear cases of great importance en banc, or they may reconsider *en banc* a case that was previously heard by a smaller panel.

How Opinions Are Published

Opinions are published chronologically in books called **reporters**. Until electronic search engines made it possible to use Boolean or other search algorithms to find cases on a particular topic, lawyers used a finding tool called a **digest** to find cases. The West Publishing Company organized the law into topics, and within each topic numbered discrete issues. A digest index provided a way to find particular topics and issues within a case — even when the case contained many issues on different topics. Today's lawyers are most likely to use digests and key numbers when searching for a topic in multiple jurisdictions. The topic and key numbers are fully functional in Westlaw. Other research product vendors, like Lexis, have developed similar indexes to issues addressed in court opinions.

"Unpublished" opinions are the subject of modern controversy. As electronic sources have increasingly replaced print sources, lawyers have gained access to opinions that in earlier times would have been inaccessible. The United States Supreme Court held in 2006 that, beginning January 1, 2007, lawyers could cite "unpublished" opinions, but the precedential value of such opinions remains a matter of debate. Currently, lawyers must check the rules of the individual jurisdiction to discover whether opinions available as "unpublished" have precedential value. A stunning paradox is that the *Federal Appendix* publishes "unpublished" opinions.

When looking for policy, look to higher courts because they create rules that will apply to a variety of cases. When looking for how to apply broader rules to specific situations, especially if the issue is fact-intensive, look to lower courts, such as the trial courts in the federal system.

Although the rules for citing cases are complex, especially those governing how to abbreviate the parties' names, the information that you must convey in a case citation is basic and easy to remember. The reader seeing a full citation must be able to discern exactly the jurisdiction that published the case, the level of the court that decided the case, the year it was decided, and the page of the case to which you refer. All of the citation information becomes important when you are judging the strength of an argument or deciding which cases to use when you write. Citation basics are covered in Appendix B.

THE BASICS YOU NEED TO KNOW

A "case" is a lawsuit.

- But we also use the word "case" to refer to the court's written opinion resolving the lawsuit. The opinion is a story — and it usually starts with a description of the events that led the people in the story to file suit or be charged with a crime. In the discussion, the court will almost always begin by setting out the general rule, then will explain why it is or is not applying that rule to the facts, or how it is changing the rule for these particular facts. Finally, the court will tell you the outcome of the case — its holding.

Cases are published in books called reporters.

- The cases in a reporter are published chronologically and not topically. Reporters are usually organized by jurisdiction, both geographically and by level of court. The beginning of cases published by commercial companies usually start with enhancements like summaries and notes that are meant to help you understand the case. Only the part written by the court is the law. This part usually begins after the name of the judge authoring the opinion.

Connections: Statutes are mandatory authority and outweigh individual court decisions. Unless a court finds that a statute violates the Constitution (or that a state statute violates that state's constitution), the court must apply the statute as written.

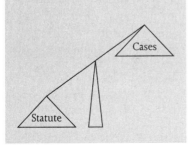

Choosing cases sometimes requires a complex analysis. But here are some guidelines:

- Choose cases from your own jurisdiction when possible. Thus, your process will involve looking first in your own jurisdiction.
- Choose cases from the highest court first and then the lower courts. Usually follow that organization in your writing as well.

- Choose cases from federal courts for issues of federal law and cases from state courts for issues of state law.
- If a statute applies, start with the statute and choose cases that interpret that particular statute.
- Choose persuasive authority when mandatory authority is unavailable to make the same point. Some persuasive authority is better than others: review the weight of authority principles in Chapter 2. If you are looking for cases that interpret a statutory provision and must turn to persuasive authority, make sure the wording of the statute the case interprets is as close to yours as possible.

Some basic places to find cases:

- Google (free) and Google Scholar (free); state court databases (free); Fastcase or Casemaker (often free with bar membership); commercial services like Westlaw, Lexis, Bloomberg, Loislaw (fee based, cost depends on plan). Appendix A will help you understand how to find cases and other authorities using different resources.

HOW IT WORKS: READING CASES AND FORMULATING RULES FROM THEM

Law school class discussions assume not only that students have read the cases, but also that they have understood them in some depth. Many different methods have been suggested for reading law school textbooks, which usually contain edited versions of cases. Reading the full text of the cases instrumentally or for the purpose of using it in written analysis is different from reading cases for law school classes.

First, you should develop and adopt an organized method for reading. After practice with the method, evaluate whether it is working for you and modify it if necessary.

Here is a relatively simple method, based on the results of a study of the reading process and strategies used by expert legal readers:

Put the case in context: Orient yourself before you read. Examine the citation. What is the name of the case? Are the parties individuals or companies? Is it a state or federal court? What is the date? What was the social and political climate of that time? Think about your purpose. Are you reading to help resolve a client's problem? Are you reading to find potential arguments? Are you reading to evaluate the court's reasoning?

Read the case flexibly for an overview. Be alert to the typical structure of cases:

> Summary of previous proceedings
> Issues or dispute
> Facts
> Rule
> Rationale or reasoning
> Decision

Understanding the facts is critical to understanding the case. Focus on the first few sentences that describe the parties and the dispute. Picture the facts. What happened? To whom? Why? Legal analysis is usually a mix of law and facts. We look to cases to see facts illustrating a rule. This illustration often tells us much about how the court will apply the rule in future cases.

Find the decision and the rule. Is the judgment reversed or affirmed, the motion denied or granted? Why? What rule of law is the judge applying? Understand the legal proceeding and the procedural posture of the case. Identify the issue. Why is this case in court? On what general legal grounds? What does the court say is the issue?

Reread the case analytically. Pause and think about the implications of words. Notice key terms and qualifying words. Define the key terms using the context or a legal or traditional dictionary. Pay attention to qualifying words (if, when, only) that may significantly alter the meaning of a sentence.

Distinguish relevant from irrelevant facts. With the issue, decision, and rule in mind, determine which facts were important to the court's decision. Often facts that are essential to one party's argument are considered to be irrelevant by the court.

Study the rationale. Separate the rationale from the dicta, the other legal rules and statements not directly involved with the decision. The rationale may contain the reasons for the rule and its application.

Synthesize the case. How do its parts fit together? How does this case fit into what you already know about this area of the law? How would you apply this rule to different facts? Monitor your understanding, as you read and after you read. Use the questions above as a self-test.[1]

Make notes or "brief" cases as a preparation for writing. As you read, make notes of the following components of the case: the facts, issue, rule, rationale and application, and the outcome of the case. Notice the general rule that the court is deciding whether or not to apply. This is the broad, general rule that existed *before* this case. This rule may be a common law rule or a statutory rule. Notes on the application will explain, in your own words, why the court applied or did not apply the rule of law to the facts in that case. Then include the specific rule, where the court decided the current case, and notice if the current case changes the general rule in any way. This is the rule that the court will apply *going forward*. Sometimes it will help to make a chart of facts and outcomes to help you synthesize how different cases address the various parts of the rule you are applying.

Form the rule. Just as lawyers expect statutory rules to follow certain patterns, the same schema will help you form rules from cases; if all the elements of the rule are present, *then* the following results must, must not, or may occur, *unless* one of the exceptions applies. Additionally, cases may set out a rule that asks the decision-maker to weigh factors, or to balance competing interests.

[1]Source: Mary A. Lundeberg, *Metacognitive Aspects of Reading Comprehension: Studying Understanding in Legal Case Analysis*, 22 READING RES. Q. 407 (1987).

Connections: Appendix A tells you some of the many ways to find applicable cases. You don't always have to start by searching directly for the case. You may find references to cases in secondary sources or cross-referenced in statutes. Your careful reading and analysis of the component parts of the rule within a case will help you discover if the case is applicable to your issue.

More Connections:

You should connect cases to:
The statute they interpret and apply.
The regulations they interpret and apply.
Mandatory precedent.

You may connect cases to:
All the other cases in the same jurisdiction on the same issue.
Cases on different issues in the same jurisdiction if you can connect the issues.
Cases from different jurisdictions on the same issue.
Cases from a secondary source by using the secondary source to understand the law.

WRITING ABOUT CASES

1. *Formulate a rule from the law and facts in the case, and break the rule into its component parts.* Sometimes you will be drawing the rules entirely from the case when you are working with the common law. Other times, you may be using cases to formulate a rule for proving just one part of the statute that applies to your case. In either case, frequently you need to use more than one case to formulate the rule; we call that *synthesizing* the rule. Whether a rule governs an entire issue, or just one part of an overarching rule, rules for cases and statutes both require careful analysis of what exactly you need to prove.

   Just as in working with rules from statutes, you should notice whether the rule is made up of elements (where you must prove them all) or factors (where the court may weigh or balance more than one part). Also check whether the component parts are mandatory, prohibitory, or discretionary. A mandatory rule tells you that someone "must" or "shall" do something. A prohibitory rule tells you that someone "must not" or "shall not" do something. A discretionary rule tells you that someone "may" do something.

2. *Legal analysis mixes rules with facts: match the rule's component parts with the facts of your legal problem.* Facts are a critically important part of case analysis. Remember that statutes provide general rules, but cases apply rules to particular facts. Often we support arguments by comparing the facts of our case to the facts of a precedent case. As you match your facts to the rule, you will see which parts of the rule will be disputed. This will help you decide how to target your further research.

3. *Most often you will organize your writing around the organization of the rule.* You will explain to your reader the parts of the rule that will be at

issue, and you'll analyze each contested component separately — usually in the same order as organized in the rule. You'll research each contested part to find the rule and the cases that apply the rule for that particular component of the overall rule.

4. *Choose precise words about cases and courts.* The wrong choice will mark you as a novice. Often you will use the same words as the rule uses, without substituting synonyms or varying your choice to make your writing more "interesting." You will also choose different words depending on the context. For example, we often use different terms when the case is about a criminal issue than we do when it is about a civil issue:

Criminal Cases	Civil Cases
guilty	liable
not guilty	not liable
prosecutor	plaintiff
accused	sued
charged	brought suit against
prosecuted a defendant	sued a defendant

Make sure the subjects of your sentences are capable of doing the action in them. Be careful about using "court" and "case" interchangeably when you're looking for the subject of a sentence. Although common usage allows you to say either "the court held" or "the case held," that usage doesn't go far. Cases don't usually "reason," "note," or "find." Courts do.

And as with statutes, you can't use *element, factor, prong,* and *condition* interchangeably. Each is a "term of art" with a precise meaning. Don't worry about repeating yourself; use the correct noun. For choosing verbs in cases, here are some examples:

Courts do:	Courts don't:
"hold" (law)	"argue"
"find" (facts)	"contend"
"note" (usually dicta)	"apply the facts" (they do "apply" rules)
"reason"	"claim"
"apply" (a rule or standard)	"assert"
"establish" (rights, duties, or rules)	"allege"
"grant" or "deny" (a motion or objections, etc.)	
"affirm" "modify" or "reverse"	

EXAMPLES AND EXPLANATIONS

Examples

I. Here are some examples of sentences students might write about cases they found. Think about each statement, what it cites to and how it characterizes the source. Evaluate whether the student has effectively presented the case.

1. The *Smith* dissent held that the trade secret plaintiff must allege a violation with sufficient particularity that the defendant can ascertain the boundaries of the secret. *Smith v. Jones*, 155 F.3d 1161, 1164 (8th Cir. 1999) (Jackson, J. dissenting).

2. The common law courts have interpreted Title VII to hold that discrimination includes using sex stereotypes to evaluate an employee. *Price Waterhouse v. Hopkins*, 490 U.S. 228, 233 (1989).

3. The *Strickland* Court held that an attorney is ineffective if his actions are so egregious they prejudice the defendant's right to a fair trial. *Strickland v. Washington*, 466 U.S. 668 (1984). The *Strickland* test is inappropriate here, however, because it applies only to post-conviction situations. *United States v. Cronic*, 466 U.S. 648, 659 (1984).

4. Although the Ninth Circuit has addressed when a "final agency action" is ripe for review, the case that this court must follow is *Colorado Coal v. Office of Legacy Management*, where the federal trial court recognized that the issuance of leases weighs in favor of finding that the action is ripe for judicial review. *Colo. Coal v. Office of Legacy Mgmt.,* 819 F. Supp.2d 1193, 1206 (D. Colo. 2011).

II. Your assignment involves common law fraud in Illinois. Describe the various factors you would take into account as you decide where to begin your research. Further describe how you would decide which sources might be most valuable to you.

III. Choose the correct answers below. More than one answer may be correct.

1. You are researching a search-incident-to-arrest issue and will be writing a brief to the United States Court of Appeals for the Third Circuit. You find a helpful opinion online that is marked "unpublished." What should you do?

   a. Cite to the opinion because it's helpful and you can use an Internet citation to help your reader find it.
   b. Do not cite to the opinion because it's "unpublished."
   c. Go to the Third Circuit's website to see the rules about unpublished opinions posted there and make your decision accordingly.

   d. Find the United States Supreme Court decision which held that
      lawyers can cite to unpublished opinions, and cite both the
      unpublished case and the Supreme Court case.

2. Forming rules:

   a. is a process of separating the parts of the rule into a list of things
      you either must prove or disprove, or factors you must weigh,
      unless there are exceptions provided, whether you are working
      with statutes or cases.
   b. is a similar process for statutes and cases, for several reasons
      including that in both situations you may need to look in more
      than one place for the pieces to put together.
   c. is easy once you find the holding of an individual case.
   d. doesn't involve worrying about the facts of a specific case.

Explanations

I.   1. Dissents don't "hold" because they are not the law. Dissents are
     persuasive authority at best. Sometimes the citation will be sufficient
     to let your reader know that you're using a dissent, which is persuasive,
     rather than the majority's rule. Often you'll want to signal that infor-
     mation in the text of the sentence as well. You might say something like
     this: "The *Smith* dissent would have fashioned a rule requiring the trade
     secret plaintiff to allege a violation with sufficient particularity that the
     defendant could ascertain the boundaries of the secret."

I.   2. The "common law" doesn't interpret Title VII, a federal statute,
     because the common law involves cases where no statute governs the
     analysis. Also, carefully choose your subject and verb when writing
     about cases. "Cases" don't "hold," but "courts" do.

I.   3. This is a helpful way to present the rules that apply to your case,
     because you will rarely draw a rule from just one case. Often you will
     need to find more than one case to form the rule, and you'll often set out
     the rules using more than one sentence.

I.   4. Federal trial courts are not binding on any other courts. Because the
     decisions are not followed by another court, they are only persuasive.
     Thus, most often you would use them to illustrate the rules set out by
     higher courts.

II. Many factors will help you determine how to proceed. And there are many
     ways you could successfully start. Some of the factors you would consider:
     Is the case based on state law or federal law? Is it civil or criminal? Is there
     an issue based on the United States Constitution? What court will decide
     the issue and what will be mandatory, primary authority in that court?
     What is the best authority? Is there a statute on point? If there is, you can

start with the statute and then search for cases interpreting it. Once you have answered these questions, you should know what the "best" authority is. Then you can determine how to look for it.

You can start with free sources and move to commercial sources only after you've exhausted free sources. You can start with a secondary source to gain background knowledge about the issue, and to find cross-references to primary sources. You can decide that as a student you should become proficient working with commercial sources while you have free access to them and start there. Remember that you should first make the decisions about what comprises the best authority rather than letting a search engine or commercial source decide what comes up at the top of your list. Whenever you begin to research, try to develop some expectations about the kind of authority that will help you answer your question.

You will then need to begin an analytical reading of the sources you find. Reading, searching, and beginning to write are all interconnected processes. Don't expect to do any of them in isolation. You'll begin to know when you have enough sources, not only because you start seeing the same sources using various searches, but also when you begin writing and have enough law to give a full picture of the state of law on a particular issue. The holes in your analysis will tell you that you are not finished researching.

III. 1. A is not a good answer. You would first need to research whether the Third Circuit encourages the use of unpublished opinions. B is similarly wrong. Check before you decide whether to use the case or not. C is a good way to approach the decision of whether to cite the case. When you read the Third Circuit's rules, you see: "The court by tradition does not cite to its nonprecedential opinions as authority. Such opinions are not regarded as precedents that bind the court because they do not circulate to the full court before filing." 3d Cir. I.O.P. 5.7. D is incomplete. Although the U.S. Supreme Court has held that lawyers can cite unpublished opinions, you would still want to know whether the particular court to which you are writing encourages this use.

III. 2. A is correct. Although the process of outlining a rule may feel different for statutes and cases, the rules you distill follow the same basic patterns. B is also correct. You often need to find several parts of a statute that have been codified in different places. And most often you'll need to use more than one case when synthesizing the most recent version of rules drawn from cases. C is incorrect because the holding of an individual case is specific to that case, and you will likely need to synthesize more than one case to state and explain a rule. D is incorrect. You sometimes need to analyze a rule in light of the facts before the court when it formed the rule. Sometimes the court will make statements about facts that are different than those before the court. These statements are dicta, and not the law.

6

Judicial Opinions in Action

Cases are stories. Often the first reading of cases is simply to understand the story — what happened, who are the characters and what are their positions in the story, and why are the characters in opposition? Cognitive scientists, narrative theorists, and old-fashioned storytellers all tell us that stories are how we understand the world. We are hardwired to make sense of text or experience through stories. Cases fill that function for us as we research. They help us understand and remember what legal rules, principles, and policies mean.

The first chapter on judicial opinions introduced you to the basics — how cases come into being, how they are published, and how you write about them. This chapter goes further — it introduces you to the complex decisions sometimes necessary when you are choosing cases to set out rules; explain rules; relate the case to statutes, regulations, or to interpret other cases; and to support arguments you make in a specific context. We'll work through two examples, going from the simple to the complex. In each case, we'll see that, similar to researching statutes, you'll need to both understand the big picture — what the opinion seeks to accomplish and how it relates to other sources — and understand how the court's application of the rule to the facts of a specific case in a specific context helps you predict how the law will apply to your case.

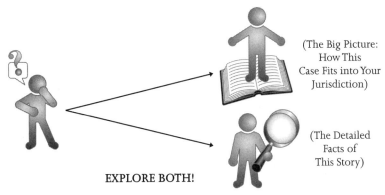

(The Big Picture: How This Case Fits into Your Jurisdiction)

(The Detailed Facts of This Story)

EXPLORE BOTH!

Before we get to our sample problems, it will help to remember some preliminary principles about research in any area you think might be governed by or explained by judicial opinions.

THE PRELIMINARIES

A short review of the steps suggested in the last chapter: As with other research, as a novice you should begin by reviewing weight of authority principles for your jurisdiction and whether federal or state law applies. Name the sources that will provide binding or mandatory authority for your case. Check to see if a statute governs, or whether the issue is governed by common law. In either case, find the rule, analyze the rule by breaking it into its component parts, and be sure you understand what you need to prove or refute. Then begin researching each piece of the rule. These preliminary steps will soon become second nature to you as you gain experience. The next steps will vary from problem to problem, as the combination of law and facts changes the way you might choose to use sources. Here are some points to remember:

Advocates may view differently the importance or value of sources in various contexts.

- Sometimes weight of authority questions can be clear. For example, when you can make the same argument using either mandatory or persuasive authority, you should always prefer the mandatory authority. If there is mandatory authority on your issue, even if it feels like a stretch to apply it, you should at least address it briefly before going to persuasive authority. But after that call, it's really hard to set out black and white answers.
- The weight and relationship among authorities is a complex calculation and one that lawyers will answer in different ways. Sometimes the weight will depend on your creativity and skill in crafting an argument from the many available choices. Some of these decisions will be easier as you gain experience creating and communicating arguments. Some decisions will always be hard—even when you have been practicing for years.

As a reminder, there are many factors to consider as you choose among persuasive authority. Here are some of those factors.

- Factual similarity and contrast between the source and your facts
- The level of the deciding court
- The date of the opinion
- Whether the opinion is well reasoned and thus more persuasive
- The reputation of the court
- Whether the issue is "of first impression" or mature in your jurisdiction

- Shared doctrines, statutes, and wording in the jurisdictions
- Shared demographic, geographic, or historic similarities in the jurisdictions
- The political reputation of the court

Ladders of Abstraction and Cases: Don't Be Too Quick to Decide a Case Doesn't Help

When you are researching for helpful cases, you will often find cases that at first glance seem factually too far afield from the facts you need to analyze to be helpful. But if you learn to move easily up and down "the ladder of abstraction," you may find ways to use cases with strong weight of authority that were not at first obviously analogous. The ladder goes from concrete to abstract. The principle is to think about the concrete facts of the case more abstractly and try to fit them into larger and more general categories so that you can find the similarities and differences you need to make analogies.

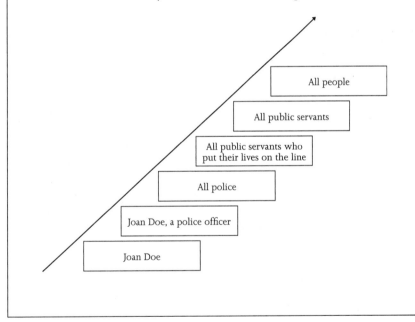

How you frame and filter a search will vary.

- If you find little authority on point, you may need to think of your issue in more abstract or general terms.
- If you find many cases on point, think more narrowly. Filters represent a way to apply the factors we just listed.

Finally, remember that researching, reading, and writing are reciprocal processes. Your research will inform your writing and your writing will tell you when you need to research more.

- If you don't stop to read and write, you will just keep piling up research that may or may not be helpful to you. Once you have a rule, whether statutory or common law, find the mandatory authority that illustrates how to apply the rule.
- Sorting is the next key action. Read and sort the cases in ways that will help you argue each part of the rule.
- When you find you lack the support you need to make an argument effectively, research some more, and move on to persuasive authority if necessary.

Now let's work through two tasks that involve researching and understanding cases.

TASK 1: WHAT'S THE RULE FOR THE TORT OF BATTERY IN WYOMING?

We start with an easy one. It's simple, but it illustrates a few traps for beginning researchers. If you follow your first instincts and do a search for "battery," whether in a commercial service or on Google Scholar, you will start to see the questions involved. First, make sure you research efficiently by limiting the search to your jurisdiction. If you just search for "battery" without narrowing the jurisdiction, a Westlaw search currently indicates that you would find 10,000 cases and 10,000 statutes. You need to narrow the search to your jurisdiction to find the law that the court must apply in your case. So the first tip for novices is to be sure you narrow the search to the Wyoming cases. Much better results: now we cut the number of cases and statutes retrieved to around 600 and 115 respectively. And we know that the statutes and cases we are reading are the best authority if we will be analyzing what will happen in a Wyoming court.

Next, if you skim through the first three or four cases, you will probably see that some of the cases indicate that one of the parties is "State," as in *Dean v. State*. And the case uses the word "guilty." You are reminded that the law recognizes two kinds of suits for battery: criminal and civil. By definition in the question above, you're looking for the tort, and not the crime. So you want to weed out all those criminal cases. The way to do that is to alter your search. Try "civil battery." Better again: we are down to 72 cases and 21 statutes. As you skim the new list, you see that some of the cases are still criminal cases, but they have the word "civil" somewhere within the opinion. So you try a variation: "tort of battery." Wyoming is a state with a small population and a fairly short history and thus not much case law. You're down to a very manageable 41 cases. Your next question is whether a statute addresses the tort of battery, or whether it is a common law tort and you need to find the rule in the Wyoming cases. When you check the Wyoming statutes, you do not find a statute for the tort of battery, only the crime of battery. Thus, you'll be reading the cases to find the rule.

Next, skim a few cases. Remember you are looking both for the big picture — what the rule is — and the detailed facts of the individual stories that illustrate how the court has applied the rule. It probably makes sense to start with a few of the most recent cases to see the rule as it is today. As you read, you may find that many of the modern cases cite an early case, where the jurisdiction first recognized a cause of action for this particular tort. If a case is often cited for the rule, and the rule hasn't changed, you'll want to make a note to cite that case.

As you read recent cases, you will sometimes see that although the case concerned the tort, the appeal was based on another issue, such as whether evidence was properly admitted, or whether the defendant is a governmental entity that might claim immunity for one reason or another. Those cases are less helpful unless you have an evidentiary question, or a governmental entity is involved in your case. But regardless of cases that concern a different issue, you should be able easily to find several cases that decided the merits of the tort claim. Those cases often set out the rule and illustrate the rule with facts.

At this point, once you know the rule, you'll begin to think about your facts and how the facts might meet the individual elements of the rule. This means you also need to start to pay attention to the facts of the precedent that illustrate how the court has applied the rule in the past. You'll be looking for facts that you can use to argue that your case is similar to or distinguishable from the precedent on certain elements. Once you have a rule, it sometimes makes sense to start making notes about which elements were at issue in a particular case. If there are elements at issue that the Wyoming court has never addressed but that might make a difference in your case, then you might widen your search to other jurisdictions. If you do widen the search to include persuasive authority, you will search narrowly for cases focusing on the particular element that the Wyoming courts have not addressed. You will hope to find a common law rule in another state that is worded very much like Wyoming's. You might consider which cases come from courts that are geographically or demographically similar to Wyoming. Or you might simply be searching broadly for facts that are very similar to your own.

As you skim through the cases, deciding which deserve a closer read, notice if certain issues reappear regularly, such as the amount of damages allowed, or how the statute of limitations applies. If you are writing for a first-year legal writing class, chances are good that your professor just wants you to analyze the merits of the battery claim, and not to be sidetracked with other issues. But regardless of your audience, you may want to make a note of those reoccurring issues and check to be sure they won't be at issue in your case.

TASK 2: ARE NEWSPAPER STRINGERS "EMPLOYEES" UNDER THE ADEA IN THE THIRD CIRCUIT?

Eugenia Green, 54, works for a small city newspaper, and believes she has been discriminated against on the basis of her age. The city is geographically within the jurisdiction of the Court of Appeals for the Third Circuit, a federal court. Twenty-two people work for the newspaper, including seven "stringers," journalists who are paid for each piece of published work. In fact, nearly all of the reporting is done by the stringers, who are all quite active. Chapter 5, Legislation in Action, described how both federal and state statutes might apply to a legal issue related to a mandatory age of retirement. That's true here, too. But here you have been asked to research federal law — whether the Age Discrimination in Employment Act of 1967 (ADEA) applies to the newspaper.

Your first step is to find the statute, the ADEA, and to read the section explaining which employers fall under it. A free Google search will give you the citation and the text of the Act. The website of the Equal Employment Opportunity Commission sets out the Act fully. The citation for the ADEA is 29 U.S.C. §§ 621 et seq. The statute begins with a congressional statement of the findings and purpose of the Act, and continues through many sections. Section 630 is devoted to definitions. There you will find the definition of an employer under the Act in § 630 (b):

> The term "employer" means a person engaged in an industry affecting commerce who has twenty or more employees for each working day in each of twenty or more calendar weeks in the current or preceding calendar year: *Provided*, That prior to June 30, 1968, employers having fewer than fifty employees shall not be considered employers. The term also means (1) any agent of such a person, and (2) a State or political subdivision of a State and any agency or instrumentality of a State or a political subdivision of a State, and any interstate agency, but such term does not include the United States, or a corporation wholly owned by the Government of the United States.

The key language for Green's purposes is that the newspaper only meets the threshold of "twenty or more employees" if the stringers are employees under the Act, and if the stringers are at work "each working day in each of twenty or more calendar weeks in the current or preceding calendar year." Whether the stringers work the required calendar days and weeks is a question of fact that you will need to document with the client. But to decide the question of whether they are "employees," the statute states "an employer" is someone with "employees." If you find this a bit of a circular definition, you are not alone. Even the United States Supreme Court found it to be circular. So we have an issue that will require research that goes beyond the statute to the cases interpreting it. We'll look to judicial opinions to tell us what it means to be an "employee."

First, you may remember from your Torts class the distinction between an employee and an independent contractor when applying the doctrine of *respondeat superior*. If you have forgotten that, a search for "are newspaper stringers employees of the paper" in either Google or commercial services such as Bloomberg, Lexis, or Westlaw will provide the reminder. You'll see both cases and secondary sources that make a key distinction between freelancers who are "independent contractors" and those who can be classified as "employees."

Now that we know some of the terminology involved, we can craft a search for cases that set out the test for whether someone is an employee or an independent contractor. Start narrowly by setting the jurisdiction as the Third Circuit, and try a natural language search for "test for independent contractor and employees age discrimination." If your search revealed nothing, you would broaden the jurisdiction, but instead, you find the search brings sixty or so cases.

Start by skimming through the results, looking for the most recent case to find the test you are seeking. The most recent cases you find may or may not be relevant to the question of who is or is not an employee. But you find a very relevant case from 2011, *Pavlik v. International Excess Agency, Inc.*, an "unreported" case. You know that you'll need to research the Third Circuit's rule on using unreported cases if you intend to cite this case to a court, but skimming through it, your eye is caught by this sentence, "Both Title VII and ADEA use the same test to determine whether an individual is an employee or an independent contractor. Nationwide Mut. Ins. Co. v. Darden, 503 U.S. 318, 322–23, 112 S.Ct. 1344, 117 L.Ed.2d 581 (1992)." Now you know to turn to the United States Supreme Court, the best possible authority interpreting federal statutes, and you have a citation to guide you.

Reading through *Darden* you find the test you need:

> Thus, we adopt a common-law test for determining who qualifies as an "employee." . . .
>
>> we consider the hiring party's right to control the manner and means by which the product is accomplished. Among the other factors relevant to this inquiry are the skill required; the source of the instrumentalities and tools; the location of the work; the duration of the relationship between the parties; whether the hiring party has the right to assign additional projects to the hired party; the extent of the hired party's discretion over when and how long to work; the method of payment; the hired party's role in hiring and paying assistants; whether the work is part of the regular business of the hiring party; whether the hiring party is in business; the provision of employee benefits; and the tax treatment of the hired party.

Now that you have found the test and know what kind of analysis you are looking for, you may want to check once more to make sure the Third Circuit hasn't explicitly decided the question of newspaper stringers. So you do a narrow search that focuses only on newspapers and stringers in the Third Circuit. The results of your search include several cases involving newspapers in other contexts — including cases like *Tinley v. Gannett*, which is about whether newspaper haulers are employees or independent contractors for the purposes of ERISA — and several cases involving stringers and the Labor Relations Board or worker compensation. But no Third Circuit case explicitly states whether stringers are employees for the purposes of the ADEA or Title VII.

Moving next to find cases that illustrate how the factors have been analyzed in the Third Circuit in other situations, you search for "Darden factors," including the quotation marks to limit your results specifically to the Darden factors and not to include other factors tests. The result is fewer than fifty cases that include many illustrations of the analysis you seek. You will read them with an eye toward sorting examples of the various factors, and thinking about the analogies you can make between newspaper stringers and the jobs at issue in these cases.

Finally, you may wish to find any case nationally that analyzes whether a stringer is an employee or an independent contractor. Using Google Scholar with a database of federal cases, you find that the First Circuit has found that newspaper stringers are independent contractors, but in the context of libel law in *Kasel v. Gannett*. Again you see an analysis of the Fair Labor Standards Act, but not an analysis of the Darden factors. But if you were struggling to make the points you want to make by analogy to the Darden factors cases, it's possible you might turn to these cases. You would juggle the factors mentioned above to decide which persuasive cases to use. Begin to write, and let the writing process send you back to research when necessary.

EXAMPLES AND EXPLANATIONS

Examples

It's always good to get some hands-on experience. Here are two questions that will allow you to practice researching cases. Law is open-ended, changing as time passes. And the tools to find law are open-ended, changing often, just like the law. Thus, the questions below are open-ended so that you can strike out on your own path without needing to replicate someone else's out-of-date research. Take our questions as a starting point and see where you go. The Explanations discuss some of the things you may see on your research path. Remember that if you need help knowing how to use various tools to search, look to Appendix A.

1. Is posting on Twitter using someone else's password "Identity Theft"? John and Joe are two friends who are actors up for the same part. John

knows Joe's Twitter password and sends out a tweet making fun of the director who is hiring for the play. Use the jurisdiction of your choice to see what you can find. What do you have to prove? If your jurisdiction returns nothing about Twitter, climb the "ladder of abstraction" to look for other social media. Is there anything in your jurisdiction that will allow you to make analogies? Move to persuasive authority. Do you find anything nationally?

2. This problem is more of a thought experiment, but you will think through the problem better if you try some simple research on your own to see what's out there. Here are the facts: A local conservation group wants to eradicate a plant that is choking the healthy plant life in a creek used as a water supply. Explore a bit online. What part would judicial opinions play in your research examining whether pesticides and herbicides are pollutants under the 1972 Clean Water Act (CWA)?

Explanations

1. As you've done before, you'll start by thinking about the legal issue, followed by reminding yourself about the hierarchy of authority in your jurisdiction. Is "identity theft" a crime? Although there may also be civil claims you could bring for damages, in most jurisdictions "identity theft" is a crime. Are there torts that would give Joe a civil cause of action to sue for damages? Perhaps. But try to stay focused on one claim at a time, and here you've been asked about "identity theft."

   Is the law likely to be federal or state? A simple Google search brings you to 18 U.S.C. § 1028A — the federal identity theft statute. But after a quick skim you see that the federal law requires a predicate offense; that is, persons can only be charged if while using the identifying information of another they also commit a felony. Our facts about Twitter most likely rule that statute out. You might investigate further to be sure, but you would most likely turn to state law.

   You will also probably run into federal statutes dealing with credit card theft and internet fraud. These possible offenses are interesting and may raise other possibilities, but we want to concentrate on the crime of identity theft.

   So try your hand at state law. Most states have several laws in the criminal code that involve taking another's identity. Maybe your Google search turned up a website where you can click on any state and see the identity theft laws. Whatever state you chose you will most likely find these elements, or a slight variation of these elements: anyone who (i) knowingly (ii) uses anyone else's personal identifying information or impersonates another, (iii) with the intent to obtain a benefit themselves or injure another has committed identity theft.

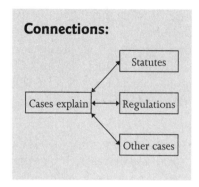

Connections:

You may find it difficult to find a specific case involving a Twitter password, but it will be easy to find examples of passwords stolen "for personal benefit" or "to injure another" within the category of "social media." And this is one of those newer areas of law where secondary sources abound that will lead you to relevant case law. Whether you research this problem as a part of a class exercise or on your own, it would be informative at this point to compare your results with a colleague who has done the same search.

2. Although you might think of the issue as "statutory" because it is based on the CWA, of course it is case law that will explain what the statute actually means. You might turn to judicial decisions for a statement of the policy behind the Act. You certainly will use case law to examine how courts have defined the text of the statute, from looking for cases that define "chemical waste" to cases that explore and expand upon the statute's definition of "pollutant."

The issue also could concern administrative law, because the Environmental Protection Agency (EPA) is likely to have promulgated regulations or other authority on when and what kind of permit might be needed to use a pesticide in a certain situation. But you might turn to case law to discover whether the EPA had the authority to adopt the regulations it issued, or to create exemptions to the Act. Or you might look at cases to decide how much deference the current court must give to the EPA rulings. And cases may help you explore if your situation is analogous to the situations the EPA had in mind when it issued its regulations and opinions.

Depending on the procedural posture of your case, you might also need authority to claim that the case is properly before the court. Issues like jurisdiction, standard of review, and whether summary judgment is appropriate will be governed by judicial opinions. Thus, even when the issue is based in statutes and regulations, judicial opinions are the great "explainers" of our law. You will find that most of your research for other sources is intertwined, connected to, and in relationship with judicial opinions.

Identifying, Reading, Understanding, and Writing About Regulations

Grizzly bears, salamanders, mountain lions, manatees, and whooping cranes. Most of us like to think of our world as one where these creatures — and many others — thrive. And we hope that our children will inhabit such a world too. Thankfully, Congress is of a like mind, and in 1973 enacted the Endangered Species Act (16 U.S.C. §§ 1531-1544), whose purpose is to encourage and "provide a program for the conservation of . . . endangered and threatened species." But nowhere in the Endangered Species Act, or any of the amendments to it, is there a mention of grizzly bears or salamanders or any of the other species that are threatened or endangered in the United States. If you think about it, how would Congress know what species need protection, other than by anecdote (which is not a particularly good basis for making decisions)? If a biologist, zoologist, or botanist serves in the ranks of Congress (although an unlikely prospect), those legislators should be busy making laws across all subjects. No member of Congress is — or should be — in the business of carefully gathering and examining data, going into the field to study animal and plant populations, and developing plans to protect species and their habitats. We need conservationists and other scientists, experts in their fields, to determine what species need protecting and to design programs to ensure their survival.

Administrative agencies serve precisely this purpose. Staffed by experts, they follow the mandates of legislators in implementing and enforcing statutes by acting in rule-making and adjudicative capacities — i.e., state and federal administrative agencies promulgate regulations that help administrators implement and enforce statutes, and they make decisions in situations where questions about enforcement arise. If you take an administrative law course in law school, you will learn about how agencies work and how they are authorized to act. For our purposes, you should recognize that administrative agencies are authorized to act by statute and that they act by making and enforcing regulations and providing guidance to the public. In this chapter we'll focus on regulations: what kinds of research questions you might expect to be answered by regulations, how to identify relevant regulations, and how to use and write about regulations as authority.

Now, back to mountain lions and whooping cranes. The Secretary of the Interior is charged by Congress with enforcing the Endangered Species Act. In fact, § 1533 of Title 16 of the U.S. Code (Conservation) directs and requires the Secretary of the Interior (and her staff) to first identify threatened and endangered species, and then to provide for their protection. The Department of the Interior fulfills the requirement set forth in the statute in many ways; the most important means employed by the agency is the promulgation of regulations that first designate species as endangered or threatened, and then protect their environments.

GLOSSARY

Administrative agency: Departments, agencies, and other groups within the state or federal executive branch of government. In the federal system, sometimes these agencies are cabinet departments like the Department of Homeland Security; sometimes they are agencies like the Social Security Administration; and at other times they are boards or commissions like the Securities and Exchange Commission and the Federal Trade Commission. All of these entities promulgate regulations.

Regulation: A rule promulgated by a state or federal agency in accordance with the applicable administrative procedure statute. Federal agencies must follow the procedures established in the Administrative Procedure Act (5 U.S.C. §§ 551-569); state agencies follow their own state's administrative procedure statute.

Proposed regulation: A rule that a state or federal agency *proposes* to adopt. Administrative agencies are usually required to publish proposed rules and make them available for public comment before finalizing them and making them effective. In the federal system, proposed regulations are published in the Federal Register; they are also available online (www.regulations.gov).

Temporary regulation: In cases of emergencies or when the public needs guidance right away, agencies make regulations effective immediately, without waiting for public input and review. When that happens, agencies pass and publish temporary rules. Temporary regulations are, in most cases, eventually replaced by permanent regulations that have gone through the public review process.

Administrative code: All of a jurisdiction's currently enforceable administrative regulations, arranged by subject matter and the agency that adopted them. The Code of Federal Regulations is the collection of current federal administrative regulations.

Enabling statutes: The statutes that give an administrative agency the authority to promulgate regulations on particular topics.

YOU NEED TO KNOW HOW IT'S MADE TO UNDERSTAND WHAT YOU ARE SEEING

Congress passes legislation that authorizes and directs agencies to take action. Sometimes that authority and those instructions are very broad. For example, Congress has authorized the Securities and Exchange Commission to "make, amend, and rescind such rules and regulations as may be necessary to carry out the provisions" of the securities acts passed by Congress (15 U.S.C. § 77s). That's a very broad mandate to the SEC. But other statutes give much more specific instruction to agencies. Although statutes give the Secretary of the Interior similarly broad authority to protect threatened and endangered species, she must also comply with more specific statutes that direct her and her staff to take particular actions. Section 5158 of Title 16 (Conservation) of the U.S. Code requires the Department of the Interior to "promulgate regulations governing fishing for Atlantic striped bass" in particular economic zones. While the Secretary and her staff have discretion in determining the types of regulations that will govern, they must pass *some* regulations that apply to fishing for the Atlantic striped bass.

Here's how it works:

Step 1:   Agencies propose regulations that are published in the Federal Register and posted on regulations.gov.

Step 2:   Interested members of the public read the proposed regulation and submit comments on it.

Step 3:   The agency considers public comments, revises the regulation to incorporate public comments (or not), then republishes the rule in the Federal Register as either another proposed regulation or a final and effective regulation.

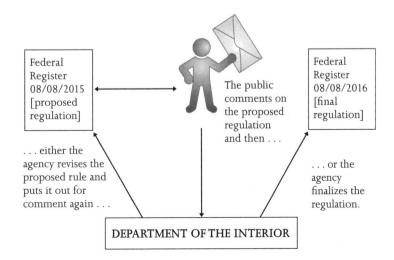

Federal Register 08/08/2015 [proposed regulation]

The public comments on the proposed regulation and then . . .

Federal Register 08/08/2016 [final regulation]

. . . either the agency revises the proposed rule and puts it out for comment again . . .

. . . or the agency finalizes the regulation.

DEPARTMENT OF THE INTERIOR

The Federal Register is published every day that the federal government is in business and includes formal actions taken by all federal agencies. Think of the Federal Register as a corollary, in an administrative law context, to the Statutes at Large (which publish, in chronological order, all legislation passed by Congress).

As regulations are finalized and published in the Federal Register, they are incorporated — or codified — into the Code of Federal Regulations ("CFR"). The CFR includes all effective regulations passed by federal administrative agencies. As regulations are added and amended, the CFR is updated. Each state also publishes its regulations in something that resembles the Federal Register and then arranges those regulations into a state administrative code.

Remember that session laws often include introductions that describe the purposes of the laws — those are called preambles. Preambles are often not codified in the U.S. Code because they do not contain binding law. Similarly, final regulations, as published in the Federal Register, include a lot of information *about* the regulations in addition to the text of the regulation itself. The Federal Register will include, among many other types of information, the agency's description and interpretation of the new or amended rule, the purposes the rule is intended to serve, the agency's reactions to public comments, and a reference to the authority by which the agency has adopted the regulation. *Only the text of the regulation itself is codified in the Code of Federal Regulations.*

Federal Register	Code of Federal Regulations
80 Fed. Reg. 68465 (Nov. 5 2015). *Disposition of Unclaimed Human Remains, Funerary Objects, Sacred Objects, or Objects of Cultural Patrimony* —Amends one regulation (43 C.F.R. § 10.2) and adopts a new regulation (43 C.F.R. § 10.7) • Summary • Background • Summary of comments • Agency response • Changes from proposed rule • Compliance with other laws • Text of amended regulation and new regulation	**43 C.F.R. Part 10:** *Native American Graves Protection and Repatriation Regulations* **43 C.F.R. § 10.2:** Definitions • Text of new and amended definitions **43 C.F.R. § 10.7:** Disposition of unclaimed human remains, funerary objects, sacred objects, or objects of cultural patrimony. • Text of new regulation

The citation 80 Fed. Reg. 68465 refers to page 68465 of volume 80 of the Federal Register.

Like the U.S. Code, the CFR is organized by title; there are 50 titles in the CFR. *Never assume that a title covering a particular topic in the U.S. Code (e.g., Title 17 – Copyrights) will correspond to a similar topic in the CFR (Title 17 – Commodity and Securities Exchanges)*. Sometimes the titles do correspond (e.g., Title 26 of the U.S. Code (Internal Revenue Code) and Title 26 of the CFR (Internal Revenue)), but it's more often *not* the case.

An administrative code for any jurisdiction—be it the CFR for our federal agencies or state administrative codes—includes all of a jurisdiction's currently effective administrative regulations, arranged by subject. Administrative codes are updated as new and amended regulations become effective. Just like a statutory code, an administrative code is divided into smaller parts. The CFR is divided into titles, chapters, parts, and sections.

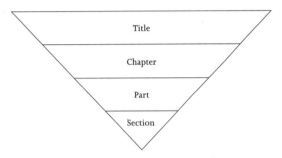

Titles within the CFR are usually further subdivided into **chapters**. For example, Title 50 of the CFR—Wildlife and Fisheries—is further divided, by subject, into six chapters. In the CFR, chapters are in turn organized into **parts**: chapters and parts reflect the agency that adopted the regulations. For example, part 17 of Title 50 of the CFR includes more than 100 regulations, all adopted by the Fish and Wildlife Service within the Department of the Interior. State administrative codes are similarly arranged hierarchically, although the name of the component parts may vary.

An administrative code section is what we normally cite when we refer to a regulation. The citation 50 C.F.R. § 17.40 refers to section 17.40 of title 50 of the Code of Federal Regulations. That section is in part 17 of Title 50.

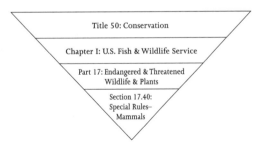

THE BASICS YOU NEED TO KNOW

Don't start your research by looking for regulations.

- Even if you think that your research question is likely to be answered by a regulation, identify the statutes that apply *before* you look at the regulations. The statute will provide context and alert you to policies and issues that the legislature considered important.

If your research question involves a statute, be sure — after you've read the statute — to see if there are regulations adopted pursuant to the statute that also apply.

- In some contexts — like tax, securities, banking, the environment, and healthcare — you can be sure that regulations apply. The more likely it is that expert input is needed to interpret and enforce legislation, the more likely that administrative regulations will be in place.

When you cite a regulation, cite its codified version in the administrative code.

- The administrative code reflects all amendments to the regulation. When you cite, for example, the Federal Register, you are citing the statement of a federal agency that includes the text of a federal regulation effective at a certain point in time.
- Sometimes you will need to look at historic versions of a regulation. Suppose your client filed a tax return in 2006 that the IRS and state taxing authorities are now examining. Rather than looking at the current version of the CFR or state administrative code to see if your client has complied with applicable tax regulations, you will need to refer to the CFR and the state administrative code as they existed in 2006.
- Regulations are amended much more frequently than statutes. As administrations change, so do approaches to regulation; as science and technology advance, new regulations supersede the old ones. Make sure that you are reading and citing either the current regulation or the version of that regulation that was effective during the time period your issue arose.

Connections: While they are very different authorities, statutes and regulations are published and organized in similar ways. Unless you are doing historical research, you will almost always cite the codes — either the statutory code or the administrative code.

Statutes at Large (federal) & state session laws
Federal Register & state administrative registers

- Publication of bills/regulations to be enacted
- Arranged in chronological order
- Never updated or amended

U.S. Code & state statutory codes
CFR & state administrative codes

- Arranged by subject
- Updated to reflect amendments
- Organized by titles (~50), chapters, & sections

Connections: Regulations cannot be enforced unless there is a statute that authorizes the administrative agency to act. Administrative regulations should always be read and interpreted in the context of the statute that authorized them. And, administrative regulations cannot go beyond what the statute authorizes. If there is ever a contradiction between an administrative regulation and the statute that authorized it, the statute controls.

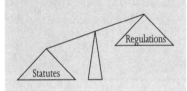

The federal government, many states, and commercial companies publish print and digital versions of current and historic administrative codes.

- These versions are — or should be — identical. But because regulations change with such frequency, you are better off looking at digital versions of the CFR and state administrative codes. The eCFR (www.ecfr.gov), the electronic Code of Federal Regulations maintained online by the federal government, is updated daily to reflect all new and amended regulations.

If statutes are hard to read and interpret, regulations can be even harder to understand.

- Regulations are authored by staff in state and federal agencies. Each agency and each administration has its own approach to drafting regulations, and it is not unusual to see very different styles of writing in administrative regulations.
- Regulations are authored by experts for experts. The language is often technical and very complex. To understand the import of a regulation, lawyers sometimes refer back to the issue of the Federal Register where the final regulation was published. The description and analysis of the regulation in the Federal Register (the preamble to the regulation) is often written in a more simple and understandable style than the regulation itself, and is a good source for information about the agency's approach to the issue and the purposes for which the regulation was promulgated. All that will help you interpret and apply the regulation.

Most litigation relating to regulations involves either a challenge to the authority of the agency to adopt the regulation or an allegation that the regulation has been improperly applied.

- Courts are more likely to find problems with a regulation than with a statute, in part because they are less deferential toward administrative agencies — which represent the current executive — than they are toward legislatures, which theoretically represent the will of the people.
- Courts can and do find that administrative agencies have overstepped the boundaries of the authority given to them by the legislature.

That's one reason why it's always important to refer to the statute as you read and interpret regulations.

- But courts also give a great deal of deference to an agency's interpretation of its own regulation. The agency's interpretation is often described in the Federal Register upon the publication of the final rule, and in guidance that the agency makes available to the public on its website or in other announcements.

Administrative agencies issue many different kinds of authorities besides regulations.

- Those authorities have different strengths and vary in nature from agency to agency.
- Administrative regulations have the force of law and are the strongest administrative authorities.
- Administrative agencies also act in adjudicative roles. Authorities issued by administrative agencies in their administrative capacity vary from agency to agency. These adjudications are usually subject to review in federal or state courts.

HOW IT WORKS: AN EXAMPLE

In 2013, the U.S. Fish & Wildlife Service (an agency within the Department of the Interior) published proposed regulations that, if finalized, would authorize the "nonlethal, incidental, unintentional take" of walruses and polar bears during oil and gas exploration activities off the coast of Alaska. 78 Fed. Reg. 1942 (Jan. 9, 2013). What is a "take"? As defined by statute (§ 1362 of the Marine Mammal Protection Act), the word "take" means to "harass, hunt, capture, or kill, or attempt to harass, hunt, capture, or kill." 16 U.S.C. §§ 1361-1423h.

You might first wonder how it is that any agency would be authorized to, in effect, allow the harassment and capture of the very animals the statute was enacted to protect. It seems a contradiction that the Fish & Wildlife Service, purportedly acting under the authority granted by the Marine Mammals Protection Act, would propose regulations that enabled the taking of walruses and polar bears. But, sadly (or not, depending on your perspective), the statute authorizes the agency to do precisely that. Section 1371 of the Marine Mammal Protection Act allows U.S. citizens to petition the Secretary of the Interior to allow them to engage in certain activities that would lead to unintentional takings of otherwise protected marine mammals. In this case, the Alaska Oil and Gas Association, on behalf of its members, requested that the Fish & Wildlife Service promulgate regulations that would allow incidental takings of polar bears and walruses in the course of oil and gas exploration activities.

In response to that request, the Fish & Wildlife Service undertook studies to evaluate the potential impact of such takings and the means to prevent harm to polar bear and walrus populations. The results of those studies, together with the agency's recommendations, constitute the proposed regulations and accompanying text published in the Federal Register on January 9, 2013. That proposal took up nearly fifty pages, although the text of the proposed regulations themselves was only a little more than four pages long. The other forty-plus pages described the studies undertaken by the agency, the need for the rule, and the agency's authority to promulgate it.

After the publication of the proposed regulations in the Federal Register, the Fish & Wildlife Service received and reviewed comments from the public. Comments on these proposed regulations reflected industry, environmental, and government concerns. Some industry commentators, like Shell Exploration & Petroleum and Conoco-Phillips, felt that the regulation did not go far enough in giving them the flexibility they needed to develop oil and gas resources. On the other side, much of the input reflected concerns about the reliability of the studies undertaken by the agency and the potentially devastating impact on marine mammal populations (these comments came from groups like the World Wildlife Fund, the National Resources Defense Council, and the Center for Biological Diversity). Some of these latter comments suggested that the agency had misinterpreted the statute and that the proposed regulations did not, in fact, comply with the requirements of the statute. Even the State of Alaska submitted comments on the proposed regulations. Input from well-recognized commenters can be very useful to a lawyer. Those comments explain — from a particular (i.e., usually one-sided) perspective — how the regulations might impact a specific industry or advocacy group. If your client's interests align with those of the comments, you can better understand the proposed regulations' effect on your client's business by reading those comments that are authored by individuals and groups that share your client's perspective.

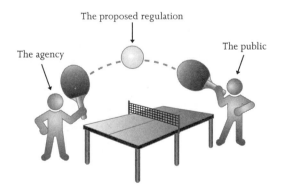

Connections: Federal (and some state) agencies maintain very rich and informative websites. For example, it's much easier to find comments on proposed federal regulations on a government website like regulations.gov than it is in a large commercial research database. Federal agency websites usually post the statutory authorities under which they operate, as well as all of the regulations, adjudications, and related materials formally or informally published by the agency. While large commercial research databases will include other types of authority, it's sometimes harder to find the informal guidance and adjudications of administrative agencies. If you know that your research involves a federal agency's actions, it's always a good idea to explore that agency's website.

Now it's the agency's turn to respond. It's a little like the back-and-forth in a game of ping pong; at any point in time, the ball is either in the agency's court or in the hands of the public. Each is reacting to what the other does. But, in the end, the agency has the bigger paddle and the stronger serve. After reviewing public input, the agency can choose to (1) revise the regulations and open them up for public comment again (and again and again and again); (2) forget the whole thing entirely; (3) finalize the rule with no changes; or (4) revise the regulations in reaction to the public comments and publish them as final (and effective) regulations.

What the Fish & Wildlife Service did in our polar bear and walrus case was the fourth option; it revised the regulations in reaction to the public comments and published them as final. Thus, six months after the publication of the *proposed* regulations, the Fish & Wildlife Service published the *final* regulations, revised to incorporate public comment, in the Federal Register (78 Fed. Reg. (June 12, 2013)). Sixty-five pages of that issue of the Federal Register are devoted to these final regulations, although the actual text of the final regulations takes up less than eight pages. The rest of the more than fifty pages (all of which constitute the preamble) describe the regulations and the science behind them and discuss the agency's decision, its reactions to the comments, and the changes to the proposed regulations. A sad outcome for the polar bears and walruses, as takings continued to be allowed, but an outcome that illustrates how the process works.

Why does this matter from a research perspective? The fifty-plus pages of agency explanation in both the proposed and final regulations contain troves of useful information for attorneys and their clients who are affected by the regulations. The agency's approach to enforcement, its interpretation of the regulations, and its understanding of its own authority are often addressed in the Federal Register versions of the proposed and final regulations. To environmental attorneys, this is a gold mine. None of this explanatory or descriptive material would be codified in the Code of Federal Regulations; only the text of the regulations themselves is in the CFR.

WRITING ABOUT REGULATIONS

In this chapter, you've learned that administrative regulations have an extraordinarily close connection to statutes. It takes an enabling statute to establish an agency and the enabling statute proscribes the limits of the agency's powers. When writing about regulations, you will find that many principles of writing about statutes also apply, especially if the agency acts in its role of creating regulations or rules.

Similarly, throughout the book we have emphasized that both the connections among sources and the context involved influence how we choose and use sources. Agencies function as promulgators of rules like statutes, but they also take on the decision-making role of courts when agencies act in their adjudicatory functions (for example, at administrative hearings). Thus, the context of whether the agency is making rules or making decisions about how rules apply becomes very important because it informs the way we write about the agency, its regulations, and its decisions.

1. *Read closely to discover the agency's role in any given situation. Pay attention to the interplay of the enabling statute, the boundaries set on the agency, and the deference the court shows the agency's actions as it addresses regulations or administrative decisions.* Once you understand what is going on, let that understanding help you frame your discussion of administrative law. If neither party questions the authority of the agency to make a particular regulation or rule, you will write about the regulation's application in nearly the same way you would write about applying a statute. But if the deference the court must show to an agency's actions is in question, the language you choose to make your arguments might be different.

For example, one of the most famous United States Supreme Court cases on the deference courts give to an agency's construction of a statute contains this statement: "Sometimes the legislative delegation to an agency on a particular question is implicit rather than explicit. In such a case, a court may not substitute its own construction of a statutory provision for a reasonable interpretation by the administrator of an agency."[1] This reminds you that before you frame the issue of your case, you will need to decide whether both parties accept the validity of the regulation that governs the issue, or if one party questions the agency's power to promulgate the particular regulation at issue. That framing will help you write the analysis of the issue.

2. *As you set up the introduction to your analysis or argument, make the relationship of the regulation to the enabling statute clear to your reader.* Quote the relevant parts of the statute and then quote the relevant parts of the regulation. Your reader will want to know precisely the text of the enabling statute that authorizes the agency to adopt the regulation in question.

3. *Just as with statutes and cases, you will need to read closely to formulate a rule and break the rule into component parts. You will use the rule, whether from a regulation or from the decision of an administrative hearing, to organize your discussion of an issue or sub-issue. Your organization may then turn to cases that interpret the regulation.* You can review these steps in either Chapter 3 or Chapter 5.

4. *Choosing precise language means you must decide whether the agency is acting in its regulatory or adjudicative role. Then choose language that reflects that role, and the fact that it is the agency acting, rather than a legislature or a court.* Agencies do "promulgate," "propose," and "adopt" regulations. They do not "enact," because they are not legislatures. When agencies hold administrative hearings, they may "determine," "decide," or "investigate."

EXAMPLES AND EXPLANATIONS

Examples

1. Read the following sentences focusing on precise word choice. Decide if each sentence needs revision.

   a. To implement Section 504, the Department of Health, Education, and Welfare has passed a regulation, 45 C.R.R. Part 84, whose key elements go beyond the spirit and purpose of the Rehabilitation Act of 1973.

   b. The regulations governing rescission of LPR status require notice be made by "personal service." 8 C.F.R. § 246.1. The definition of personal service includes service by "certified or registered mail, return receipt requested." 8 C.F.R. § 103.5a(a)(2)(iv). The same

---

1. *Chevron, U.S.A., Inc. v. Natural Resources Defense Council,* 467 U.S. 837, 844 (1984).

regulations define "routine service" as mailing a copy by "ordinary mail," expressly differentiating between the two forms of service. 8 C.F.R. § 103.5a(a)(1).

c. The Departments of Justice and Homeland Security propagated a new regulation, 8 C.F.R. § 245(a)(1), which was made effective immediately without a notice and comment period on the ground that the rules were about "agency practice and procedure," and that there was "good cause" to do so consistent with 5 U.S.C. § 553(d) because the rules were "interpretive only."

2. Evaluate the following statements about researching administrative law. Are they correct?

   a. If the regulation is the rule in your case, you don't need to worry about other authority.
   b. If the regulation is the rule in your case, you would use the Federal Register just to get the precise language of the regulation.
   c. Cases are more important than regulations.
   d. Once you find a federal regulation that governs a situation, you don't need to look for other regulations.

3. In an online commercial legal research database, you will see "credits" following the text of a statute or regulation. Those credits give the statute's or regulation's history, showing when the statute was originally enacted or the regulation first promulgated, as well as all of the amendments to the statute or regulation. The credits that appear at the end of one of our polar bear and walrus regulations (50 C.F.R. § 18.111) look like this:

   39 Fed. Reg. 7262 (Feb. 25, 1974); 53 Fed. Reg. 24283 (June 28, 1988); 54 Fed. Reg. 40348 (Sept. 29, 1989); 55 Fed. Reg. 14978 (April 20, 1990); 78 Fed. Reg. 35420 (June 12, 2013)

   Evaluate the following sentences. Are they correct?

   a. The Federal Register citations in the credits are to the proposed and final regulations published by the Fish & Wildlife Service.
   b. The most important Federal Register citation is the first one, where the regulation was originally adopted.

4. Sometimes enabling statutes give very broad authority to an agency (e.g., the SEC is authorized to promulgate "such rules and regulations as may be necessary to carry out the provisions" of the securities statutes); sometimes the authority is much narrower (e.g., the legislative direction to the Secretary of the Interior to adopt regulations governing Atlantic striped bass fishing). Think about arguments you might make that an agency has exceeded its authority in promulgating a regulation. How would those arguments differ, depending on whether the enabling statute's grant of authority was broad or narrow?

Explanations

1. (a)   The first sentence should clarify that "Section 504" refers to a section of the U.S. Code. This sentence uses the phrase "passed a regulation" which incorrectly implies that a legislative body voted on the regulation. Agencies "adopt" or "promulgate" rather than "enact" or "pass." You would also want to be careful about the word "element," which we reserve for those components of a rule that are mandatory to prove the claim. The content of this sentence, however, is an example of a plaintiff questioning whether the agency had the authority to adopt the regulation.

1. (b)   This is a good example of writing about a regulation when the authority of the agency to regulate in this particular way is not in question. In situations like these, the regulation functions just as a rule from a statute or case would. And just as with statutes, legal readers like to see the precise language of the rule, so the author has quoted the relevant parts of the regulation.

1. (c)   The word "propagate" is a poor choice here and the author probably meant to use "promulgate," the word we typically use when agencies set out regulations. The rest of the sentence makes sense. The argument that the agency failed to follow correct procedures, including allowing for a period of "notice and comment," is also a common one. You should probably note, however, if this is a temporary regulation (as almost all regulations that are promulgated without a notice and comment period are).

2. (a)   Of course this is a silly statement! First, you would always want to know about the enabling statute that gave the agency the authority to promulgate the regulation. Reading the enabling statute would help you decide whether to accept the regulation as the rule, or to argue that the agency had overstepped its authority. You would also want to look for cases that apply and interpret the regulation. Remember that regulations can be hyper-technical, so you might decide to find secondary sources, whether in print or electronic, that would help you understand the regulation.

2. (b)   It is true that you will need the precise language of the regulation, but it is the Code of Federal Regulations that will set forth its current text. The Federal Register entries for both the proposed and final rule, however, will be very helpful! The preambles might have a statement of policy and purpose. Remember the fifty-plus pages of information on the regulations about polar bears and walruses. You might find, in the Federal Register, the agency's approach to enforcement, its interpretation, and its understanding of the extent or limits of its authority to make the regulation. All of these may provide support for the arguments you want to make or answer.

2. (c)   This takes us back to our first chapters on weight of authority. Remember that it is difficult to say that one source is always more important than another. If the issue you are researching includes whether the agency was within its authority when it created a regulation, cases will most likely decide that issue. One of the recurring ideas in research is that the weight and utility of the sources you find will vary with the context in which you're doing your research.

2. (d)   Remember that regulatory schemes are often just as elaborate or more elaborate than the enabling statutes that gave rise to them. Often the statute sets out broader rules, and it is the agencies that fill in the details of enforcement by adopting specific regulations. You will need to look at the entire regulatory scheme. It's often the case (as with statutes) that definitions and exceptions to rules established in one regulation are set forth in other regulations.

    Also, don't forget that both federal agencies and state agencies promulgate regulations. It may be that your professor or supervisor has limited your research to either federal or state issues, but when you have been asked to research all possible claims, then you'll need to check both federal and state sources.

3. (a)   The citations to the Federal Register in the credits are only to the final regulations and not to proposed regulations. Proposed regulations have no binding authority, and so, are not cited in the credits. Proposed regulations may be very different from the regulations that eventually are finalized and made effective.

3. (b)   Remember that regulations may change frequently. The most important Federal Register entry will be the most recent one that reflects substantive amendments. If we think about how quickly science and technology evolve, the rationale behind an environmental regulation that was originally adopted in 1974 is likely to have changed a great deal by 2013. To understand the currently effective regulation, look at the preamble to the final regulation most recently adopted.

4. If you want to argue that an agency has exceeded its authority when its grant of authority is very broad, you will need to suggest that the agency has promulgated regulations that contravene the policies behind the statute. If the agency has authority to do basically anything that implements the statute, you'll have to argue that what the agency has done does not, in fact, further the goals sought to be achieved by Congress.

    If, on the other hand, the agency has promulgated regulations pursuant to a very narrow grant of authority, it's harder to argue that the agency is not pursuing the statute's policies. But it is easier to suggest that the agency has exceeded its particularly limited authority.

Regulations (and Other Administrative Law Authorities) in Action

Putting regulations to work—in either a litigation setting or a transactional one—is all about building. In some situations, the focus is solely on a particular regulation and its interpretation. But it's more often the case that, in an area of the law dominated by regulations, an attorney constructs an argument by hammering together a variety of authorities, from statutes and regulations to other administrative authorities and cases. In a transactional context, attorneys advise clients to help them create a framework for the future—a structure that will weather the storm and protect a business or an individual from the uncertainties of the economy and government regulation.

Any building project requires materials that serve different purposes. Suppose, in a litigation context, that a client is alleged to have disposed of hazardous materials in violation of a particular federal or state regulation. As that client's attorney, as you try to make a case that your client did not in fact violate the law, you are likely to incorporate many different types of authorities—from a statute that might describe the types of prohibited activities and a regulation that defines hazardous materials to cases that describe similar disposals and administrative rulings or reports that provide guidance on what can and cannot be done.

In a transactional context, you might represent a company that is developing procedures for its staff to follow in managing hazardous waste (to avoid the litigation that your other client is involved in!). Again, the substance of those procedures will depend on your careful reading of all of the applicable authorities and your weaving them together to create a pathway for employees to follow that will ensure ongoing compliance with the law.

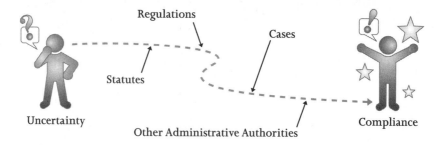

In both litigation and transactional contexts, the statute is the foundation. The previous chapter discussed the relationship between statutes and regulations. If the foundation doesn't support the building, it doesn't matter how attractive and artful that building might be; it will fall down eventually. Every regulation depends on the enabling statute. In a litigation context, you might want to argue that the statute does not support the regulation because the administrative agency has exceeded its statutory authority in promulgating it. In a transactional context, you will want to use statutes, regulations, cases, and other authorities to create a framework that supports your client's needs and protects her going forward.

After reading the first chapter on regulations, you have an idea of how regulations are promulgated and how they relate to the statute that authorizes the agency to adopt them. This chapter will help you understand how regulations, and other administrative authorities, fit into the framework of a legal argument or the construction of a transaction. We'll work through two examples — one fairly simple, the other more complex — that will illustrate the use of regulations in situations that a practicing attorney might face.

But, first, keep in mind some principles that apply in any research and writing project in an area where administrative authorities play an important role.

THE PRELIMINARIES

Begin your analysis with the language of the statute.

- Even if you know that your research problem depends upon the interpretation of a particular administrative regulation, begin by reading the statute that authorizes the regulation or otherwise relates to it.
- The statute may highlight important policies that will help you determine whether a regulation furthers those policies or contravenes them. If it contravenes them, you could argue that the agency exceeded its authority in promulgating the regulation.

- The statute may also suggest how a particular regulation should be interpreted (i.e., so that it furthers the policies important to the legislature).

Regulations are mandatory authority in the jurisdiction in which they are promulgated.

- Unless you can argue that an agency has overstepped its authority in adopting a regulation or that the regulation contravenes the intent of the statute that authorizes it (more on that in the Connections box on page 101), *regulations are mandatory authority.*
- Regulations adopted by federal administrative agencies are mandatory authority across the United States, and regulations promulgated by state agencies are mandatory in the state in which they were adopted.

Judicial decisions may interpret regulations and apply them to specific circumstances.

- Whether or not those judicial decisions are mandatory authority depends on a combination of factors — including the jurisdiction in which the case was decided, the level of the court making the decision, and the similarity of the facts.

In researching and writing about the law in any area governed by regulations, always start with the statute. Then, find regulations that implement the statute.

- Cases (which may or may not be mandatory authority) that interpret both the statute and regulations can help you understand how those authorities are applied.
- Other authorities and publications issued by the agency (which are likely not mandatory) indicate the agency's approach in implementing the statute and regulations.
- In an area dominated by regulations, don't begin your research by looking for case law. Get your footing in the statute and regulations and try to understand the regulatory scheme.
- Secondary authorities, such as treatises, can introduce you to a statutory and regulatory system and help point you to relevant primary authorities.

Administrative agencies provide written guidance, issue rulings on requests, describe their policies and procedures, and announce interpretations and enforcement plans.

- Administrative agencies publish rulings on questions that come before them, they provide formal and informal guidance to consumers on compliance issues, they respond to concerns expressed by legislators and members of the public, and they take action against individuals and companies that they think have violated regulations.

- These rulings and publications are usually not binding, except on the individual to whom they are addressed. For example, a private letter ruling from the Internal Revenue Service to a taxpayer that responds to the taxpayer's request can be relied upon by the taxpayer, but not by others.

- Non-binding administrative authorities are still valuable. Courts often defer to the expertise of the agency as expressed in those authorities, and compliance with those authorities will help you build a stronger structure for your client's activities.

If you are advising your client about how to structure a transaction or achieve a desired goal in an industry or area dominated by regulations, you'll need to read a variety of authorities — primary and secondary — to piece together an approach that complies with the statute and regulations and that conforms to the agency's interpretation of those authorities.

- Administrative publications other than regulations can be very helpful in these contexts. In responding to questions from industry and the public, and in publishing guidance and other information, the agency may indicate techniques and structures that will ensure compliance with its regulations, and provide some certainty as to how a particular legal approach will be treated by the agency.

- But, *be careful!* As administrations change (from Bush 1 to Clinton, and Bush 2 to Obama), so do agencies and their approach to enforcement. It may be dangerous to rely on a non-binding authority (i.e., *not* a regulation) issued by an agency in the distant (or sometimes not-too-distant) past.

An administrative agency's website is often a very good — and reliable — source of information about the statutes and regulations that apply in a particular industry or that govern particular types of activities.

- Agency websites often include citations to — and usually the full text of — applicable sections of the U.S. Code and the Code of Federal Regulations.

- Agency websites also include agency publications, letter rulings, notices, and other documents that can be helpful in ascertaining the agency's approach to interpreting and enforcing its regulations.

Connections: Agencies sometimes promulgate regulations as specifically directed by statute. At other times, agencies get their authority to adopt regulations from a very broad grant of authority in the statute. *If your goal is to argue that a regulation is unenforceable or that it should not be applied to your client's situation,* look carefully *at the statute that authorized the agency to promulgate the regulation.*

Specific grant of authority: *When the authority delegated by statute to the agency is specific, it is more difficult to argue that an agency was not authorized to adopt a regulation* that conforms to the statute.

Example: A section in the Internal Revenue Code (i.e., a statute) allows manufacturers of tobacco products to "furnish" those products to employees without paying the taxes that normally apply to cigarettes and other tobacco products "in such quantities, and in such manner as the Secretary [of the Treasury] shall by regulation prescribe."

• With that statutory grant of authority, it would be next to impossible to argue that the Department of the Treasury was not authorized to promulgate regulations that established a maximum amount of cigarettes that could be given to employees without payment of tax.

• But, if the regulation *entirely prohibited* any cigarettes from being given by the manufacturer to its employees without payment of the tax, then the Department of the Treasury would have overstepped its authority, and you could argue that the regulation was invalid.

Broad grant of authority: *When an agency adopts a regulation under a broad grant of authority, it's easier to suggest that a particular regulation is not contemplated by the statute and, in fact, contravenes the statute's policies.*

Example: Title 23 of the U.S. Code is titled "highways," and in § 101 of that title, Congress declared that "it is in the national interest to preserve and enhance the surface transportation system to meet the needs of the United States for the 21st Century." In § 315 of Title 23, Congress also authorized the Secretary of Transportation to "prescribe and promulgate all needful rules and regulations for the carrying out of the provisions of this title."

• Suppose the Department of Transportation adopted a regulation that *prohibited* improvements to highways that served rural communities whose populations did not exceed 250,000 people. An attorney representing a city whose population was less than 250,000 could certainly argue that the regulation is unenforceable as it does not further the policies explicitly stated in the statute.

Now let's work through two tasks that trigger research in regulations and other administrative agency authorities.

TASK 1: CAN I PREVENT MY CLIENT FROM BEING DEPORTED?

Suppose that the family of a young woman who is a lawful permanent resident of the United States (albeit not a citizen) has asked you to represent her in immigration proceedings. The Department of Homeland Security undertook removal proceedings against your potential client, alleging that she claimed to be a citizen of the United States on documents submitted to a state licensing agency. Because she was disruptive at the deportation hearing, the Immigration Judge ordered her removed from the proceedings. Her family was not in contact with her at the time of those proceedings and she was not represented by counsel. The Immigration Judge found against your client and ordered that she be deported. Finally alerted to her plight, the client's family has come to you to see if there is anything you can do to stop the deportation. Her mother and father both mention their concerns about the young woman's mental competency.

Immigration is, of course, governed by federal statutes. Sections of a treatise on immigration that cover deportation of persons lawfully in the United States would likely be helpful as a first step. A reliable secondary source should point you to Title 8 of the U.S. Code (Aliens and Nationality) and its subchapter on immigration. Part IV of that subchapter is titled "Inspection, Apprehension, Examination, Exclusion, and Removal" and sections 1227 through 1231 govern removal. From what we know about legislation, it's good to get an overview of the statutory scheme.

Title 8 of the U.S. Code

§ 1227. Deportable Aliens
§ 1228. Expedited Removal of Aliens Convicted of Committing Aggravated Felonies
§ 1229. Initiation of Removal Proceedings
§ 1229a. Removal Proceedings
§ 1229b. Cancellation of Removal; Adjustment of Status
§ 1229c. Voluntary Departure
§ 1230. Records of Admission
§ 1230. Detention and Removal of Aliens Ordered Removed

Some sections of the statute (for example, §§ 1227, 1229, and 1229a) require careful reading, while others can safely be put to the side for now. Your first task would be to determine whether the United States has grounds to deport your client. Basing the deportation decision on her statement that she was a citizen of the United States seems flimsy. But, unfortunately for your client, § 1227(3)(D)(i) authorizes deportation of a permanent resident upon a representation that she is a citizen of the United States made in order to obtain benefits under federal or state law. Another section of the statute, § 1229, provides that permanent residents may be represented by counsel in deportation proceedings. And § 1229a describes the rights of the permanent resident in any deportation hearing, including her right to be present. That section provides that:

> If it is impracticable by reason of an alien's mental incompetency for the alien to be present at the proceeding, the Attorney General shall prescribe safeguards to protect the rights and privileges of the alien.

Although there may be several grounds on which to challenge the deportation, you decide to focus first on the issue of your client's removal from the proceedings and her mental competency, and whether the safeguards required by § 1229a were in place to protect your client.

Now that you've read the statute, it's time to turn to regulations promulgated by the Department of Justice to see if they provide guidance on the nature of the safeguards to which your client is entitled.

Immigration regulations are found in Title 8 ("Aliens and Nationality") of the Code of Federal Regulations; part 1240 of Title 8 is titled "Proceedings to Determine Removability of Aliens in the United States." Finding this part of Title 8 of the C.F.R. should be fairly easy — you might do a quick Internet search for deportation regulations, refer to a reliable secondary source, or scan the table of contents of Title 8. Luckily, part 1240 of Title 8 contains a manageable number of regulations. Only a small number of those regulations might apply to the questions you are researching: (1) the removal from the deportation proceedings of a possibly mentally incompetent permanent resident and (2) the safeguards required by the statute to ensure fairness in those circumstances.

Part 1240 of Title 8 of the Code of Federal Regulations

§ 1240.1 Immigration Judges
§ 1240.1 Service Counsel
§ 1240.3 Representation by Counsel
§ 1240.4 Incompetent Respondents
§ 1240.5 Interpreter
§ 1240.6 Postponement and Adjournment of Hearing
§ 1240.7 Evidence in Removal Proceedings Under Section 240 of the Act
§ 1240.8 Burdens of Proof in Removal Proceedings
§ 1240.9 Contents of Record
§ 1240.10 Hearing
§ 1240.11 Ancillary Matters, Applications
§ 1240.12 Decision of the Immigration Judge
§ 1240.13 Notice of Decision
§ 1240.14 Finality of Order
§ 1240.15 Appeals

The most important regulation on your issue is § 1240.4. Section 1240.3 merely states that your client may be represented at the deportation hearing, and § 1240.10 describes what must happen in the hearing. Section 1240.10 may be very important to your client on other issues, but for the purposes of determining whether the safeguards required by the *statute* (8 U.S.C. § 1229a) were available to your client, it is § 1240.4 of the *regulations* (8 C.F.R. § 1240.4) that may help. The regulations promulgated by the Department of Justice indicate how the requirements of the statute are implemented.

Section 1240.4 states that:

> When it is impracticable for the respondent to be present at the hearing because of mental incompetency, the attorney, legal representative, legal guardian, near relative, or friend who was served with a copy of the notice to appear shall be permitted to appear on behalf of the respondent. If such a person cannot reasonably be found or fails or refuses to appear, the custodian of the respondent shall be requested to appear on behalf of the respondent.

Statute (8 U.S.C. § 1229a): Permanent resident has a right to be present at a hearing. Attorney General *shall establish safeguards* for residents who cannot be present because of mental incompetence.	Those safeguards are established by adoption of a regulation.	Regulation (8 C.F.R. § 1240.4): If permanent resident cannot be present because of mental incompetence, representatives may or shall appear on behalf of the permanent resident.

You've identified what *should* happen when a potentially mentally incompetent permanent resident is unable to be present at a deportation hearing. You now need to determine what *did* happen and whether any steps were taken to comply with the regulation (8 C.F.R. § 1240.4). Moreover, now would be the time to look at case law that construes the regulation and explore whether either the Department of Justice or the Department of Homeland Security, also tasked with immigration enforcement, has published rulings or guidance on the topic of mentally incompetent permanent residents who face deportation.

TASK 2: HOW CAN ENID SELL SHARES OF HER COMPANY'S STOCK?

When we last left Enid back in Chapter 4, she needed to raise money to develop her smartphone app. She had formed a corporation and you had determined that she might be able to sell shares of that corporation's stock in order to raise those funds. Enid is thinking about using crowdfunding, and you had begun to explore whether the federal securities laws (codified in Title 15 of the U.S. Code) might permit that kind of transaction. What you learned — after consulting reliable secondary sources and carefully reading the relevant statutes — was that ordinarily sales of shares of stock (a kind of security) require registration of the shares with the Securities and Exchange Commission. Registration with the SEC is a time-consuming and expensive process suitable for only the biggest and most well-funded of corporations; it's not something that Enid could afford to pursue.

Luckily, back in Chapter 4, you found that the federal securities statutes also provide exemptions from the registration requirements. Section 77d(a)(2) ("Exempted Transactions") of Title 15 of the U.S. Code provides that "transactions . . . *not involving any public offering*" are exempt from the registration requirements of the federal securities laws. Since Enid has a number of friends and family members who want to invest in her corporation, you decide to focus on that exemption. But, since Enid keeps harping on crowdfunding, you will also check to see if there are any exemptions that apply to sales of shares on a crowdfunding platform. Remember that you are trying to determine how best to accomplish Enid's goals — to raise money so that the corporation can develop and market her smartphone app.

Although the statute establishes an exemption from the registration requirements for those sales of securities that do not involve a public offering, the statute is not very helpful in describing what is and isn't a public offering. The risks of engaging in an offering that turns out *not* to be private and for which the exemption is *not* available are high. You want to make sure you get this right, so your first step in researching the private offering exemption is probably to turn to a secondary source written by a securities expert and written for the practicing lawyer. Evaluate the secondary source by considering the expertise of the author, the extent to which the source cites primary authorities, the thoroughness with which it addresses the topic, the reputation of the publisher, and all of the other factors described in Chapter 10.

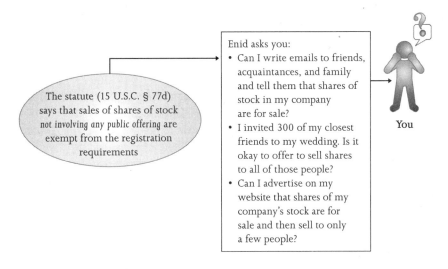

The statute (15 U.S.C. § 77d) says that sales of shares of stock not involving *any public offering* are exempt from the registration requirements

Enid asks you:
- Can I write emails to friends, acquaintances, and family and tell them that shares of stock in my company are for sale?
- I invited 300 of my closest friends to my wedding. Is it okay to offer to sell shares to all of those people?
- Can I advertise on my website that shares of my company's stock are for sale and then sell to only a few people?

You

Any secondary source that describes the private offering exemption will include a discussion of something called "Regulation D." Even a quick Google search will retrieve the Securities and Exchange Commission website that describes the non-public exemption and Regulation D. The regulations promulgated by the SEC are published in Title 17 of the Code of Federal Regulations. Remember that titles in the United States Code often do *not* correspond to titles in the Code of Federal Regulations. The securities *statutes* are in Title 15 of the U.S. Code; the securities *regulations* are in Title 17 of the C.F.R.

Despite its name, Regulation D is not one, but several regulations promulgated by the SEC to provide a means for companies to take advantage of the non-public offering exemption established by statute. Regulation D is what we call a safe harbor. Because the statute lacks detail in its description of the non-public exemption, the SEC promulgated regulations that instruct companies on exactly how to conduct a private offering and sell shares of stock, and to ensure the availability of the private offering exemption.

Regulation D is really a road map for non-public sales of shares of stock that will qualify for the exemption from registration.

Regulation D appears as rules 500 through 508 of Part 230 of Title 17 of the C.F.R.

Part 230 of Title 17 of the Code of Federal Regulations

§ 230.500 Use of Regulation D

§ 230.501 Definitions and Terms Used in Regulation D

§ 230.502 General Conditions to be Met

§ 230.503 Filing of Notice of Sales

§ 230.504 Exemption for Limited Offerings and Sales of Securities Not Exceeding $1,000,000

§ 230.505 Exemption for Limited Offers and Sales of Securities Not Exceeding $5,000,000

§ 230.506 Exemption for Limited Offers and Sales Without Regard to Dollar Amount of Offering

§ 230.507 Disqualifying Provision Relating to Exemptions Under §§ 230.504, 230.505 & 230.506

§ 230.508 Insignificant Deviations from a Term, Condition, or Requirement of Regulation D

Regulation D includes three exemption provisions (§§ 203.504, 203.505, and 203.506): which one you use depends on how much money your client wants to raise. To qualify for any of the exemptions, a sale of shares of stock must comply with the conditions set forth in § 230.502; a notice must be filed as provided in § 230.503; and there may be circumstances (as described in § 230.507) that will make the exemption unavailable. So that you can advise Enid competently, you will need to read almost all of the sections within Regulation D. Don't forget the definitions regulation (§ 230.501) — those definitions will apply throughout all the sections of Regulation D.

Enid's questions may be answered by a close reading of §230.502 (conditions to be met). But it's conceivable that, even after thoroughly and carefully reading all of Regulation D, you'll still need clarification. Now would be the time to look at other administrative materials published by the SEC and case law to determine if they can shed any additional light on how the SEC enforces Regulation D and how the courts interpret it.

But don't forget Enid's original question: can she sell her shares — without registration — through some sort of crowdfunding arrangement? One answer is to look to Regulation D — if she can fit her crowdfunded sale of shares of stock into the conditions of Regulation D, then there's nothing stopping her from taking that route. But, if the conditions set forth in § 230.502 prohibit the kind of activities that would be involved in a crowd-funded sale (e.g., advertising on the Internet), then Enid will have to find another exemption or register the shares.

Crowdfunding is a relatively new phenomenon, so you might want to start with a quick Internet search and see if you can find a reliable source of information about crowdfunding and sales of securities. And, sure enough, you will almost immediately find an SEC announcement about a newly promulgated (as of late 2015) group of regulations — titled "Regulation Crowdfunding" — that will allow companies to sell shares of their stock on crowdfunding platforms.

Regulation Crowdfunding, which appears as Part 227 of Title 17 of the C.F.R., consists of the following twenty sections:

Part 227 of Title 17 of the Code of Federal Regulations

Subpart A — General
§ 227.100 Crowdfunding Exemption and Requirements
Subpart B — Requirements for Issuers
§ 227.201 Disclosure Requirements
§ 227.202 Ongoing Reporting
§ 227.203 Filing Requirements and Form
§ 227.204 Advertising
§ 227.205 Promoter Compensation
Subpart C — Requirements for Intermediaries
§ 227.300 Intermediaries
§ 227.301 Measures to Reduce Risk of Fraud
§ 227.302 Account Opening
§ 227.303 Requirements with Respect to Transactions
§ 227.304 Completion of Offerings, Cancellations and
      Reconfirmations
§ 227.305 Payments to Third Parties

Subpart D — Funding Portal Regulation
§ 227.400 Registration of Funding Portals
§ 227.401 Exemption
§ 227.402 Conditional Safe Harbor
§ 227.403 Compliance
§ 227.404 Records to Be Made and Kept by Funding Portals
Subpart E — Miscellaneous Provisions
§ 227.501 Restrictions on Resales
§ 227.502 Insignificant Deviations from a Term, Condition or
    Requirement of this Part
§ 227.503 Disqualification Provisions

This is a far more complicated group of regulations than Regulation D. In addition to requirements that sellers of stock must meet, there are ongoing reporting requirements for sellers, as well as conditions that the crowdfunding portals must satisfy. Moreover, since this is a relatively new group of regulations, there will be few other authorities — such as guidance or rulings from the SEC or case law — that will help you flesh out the meaning and application of the new regulations. By contrast, Regulation D has been around for quite a while. There is plenty of case law and administrative material that will help you to interpret and apply its provisions.

As you counsel Enid and try to structure a framework for her company's growth, you now have two options available to you — the Regulation D exemption and the crowdfunding alternative. You can imagine Regulation D as the simple, yet well-built structure; the regulations are relatively straightforward and there are lots of other authorities to buttress your interpretation of them. Regulation Crowdfunding, on the other hand, is the sexy and sleek design that will be expensive and a little risky to build, but might be much more fun to live in.

EXAMPLES AND EXPLANATIONS

Examples

1. A new potential client, Harry, has handed you a warning letter addressed to him from the Food & Drug Administration. Harry runs a small business selling — on the Internet — what he describes as "essential oils that relieve stress, moisturize the skin, and help reduce the appearance and irritation of rashes and blemishes." The letter from the FDA refers to marketing materials produced by Harry and claims that Harry, in selling

his essential oils, has failed to comply with federal statutes and regulations that govern the sale and manufacture of cosmetics and drugs. The letter instructs Harry to take corrective action immediately or else risk legal action, including, "without limitation, seizure and injunction."

How would you approach — from a research perspective — Harry's problem?

2. Think about the following statements. Are they true?

   a. Regulations are not as important as statutes, and it is easier to get around a regulation than it is to avoid a statute.
   b. Once you find a regulation that is directly on point, you should focus on that regulation, together with the case law and administrative publications that interpret it.
   c. If there is both a state regulation and a federal regulation on a particular subject, the federal regulation is more important.
   d. If you are in the Fifth Circuit and both a Fifth Circuit opinion and a federal regulation apply to your issue, the decision of the Fifth Circuit is a stronger authority than the regulation.

3. The Americans with Disabilities Act provides that employers must sometimes make reasonable accommodations for employees with disabilities. Where is the term "reasonable accommodations" defined?

4. Suppose you are writing to the Internal Revenue Service about your client's tax problems and you ask the IRS to provide guidance to you and your client. How could the following paragraph in that letter be improved?

   The Internal Revenue Code allows taxpayers to deduct expenses related to a taxpayer's business. There are also regulations enacted by the Internal Revenue Service that provide additional deductions for travel expenses connected to a business. My client claimed a deduction for travel-for-business expenses under the regulation, rather than under the statute.

Explanations

1. There's no single way of approaching any research question. What follows is one approach that will work equally well in other contexts where regulations — and the agencies that enforce them — play an important role.

   It's likely that the letter from the FDA will identify the statutes and regulations Harry allegedly violated. In order to take corrective action, Harry will need to know the applicable law. A good place to start your research would be the FDA website. Agency websites often include descriptions of the enabling statute, as well as of the regulations that the agency has adopted and enforces. Reading an agency website can inform you about the overall regulatory scheme and provide context; it will help you to be much more efficient when you turn to a careful reading of the primary authorities.

The FDA has alleged that Harry's essential oils are subject to regulation as both cosmetics and drugs. As its website indicates, the FDA gets at least some of its authority to act from the Federal Food, Drug, and Cosmetics Act, and so, your first step would be to see if that statute defines the terms "drug" and "cosmetic," and then to determine if Harry's essential oils fall within those definitions. Section 321 of the Federal Food, Drug, and Cosmetics Act is the definitions section, and it defines both "drug" and "cosmetic." If those definitions are ambiguous or very general, then you would look to regulations promulgated by the FDA to see if the regulations clarify the statute's definitions. Determining whether Harry's essential oils fall within either or both of those definitions is the first question you should address.

If you conclude, after a careful reading of the definitions, that Harry's essential oils are neither drugs nor cosmetics, you should look to other administrative pronouncements of the FDA and case law to see if there is additional authority to support your analysis. If, on the other hand, you find it hard to argue that the definitions do not include Harry's oils, then you'll need to understand how the FDA regulates drugs and how it regulates cosmetics. That is likely to involve a careful reading of first the statute and then the regulations. You will need to determine if Harry has failed to comply with those authorities, and if so, what he needs to do to correct that failure to comply. Again, FDA publications and case law may help you interpret and apply the regulations.

2. (a) Statutes and regulations are both mandatory authority, so it's hard to say that one is more "important" than the other. It's true that regulations could not be promulgated without some legislative action (i.e., a statute) that gives authority to the administrative agency. On the other hand, much legislation could not be implemented without the adoption of regulations by an administrative agency. Violations of regulations can cause just as much trouble and expense for your client as violations of statutes. And, regulations often provide road maps to compliance and provide certainty.

Whether it's easier to "get around" a regulation than a statute is debatable. What is true is that you may argue that a regulation, unlike the governing statute, cannot be enforced either because it is not authorized by the statute or because it contravenes the statute's policies.

(b) If you find a regulation that is directly applicable to your issue, you should, of course, focus on that regulation and on other authorities — like case law and administrative agency materials — that interpret and apply it. But it's a rare regulation that is independent of the regulations that surround it and the statute that authorizes it. In reading any one regulation, you will need to keep in mind and often refer back to the enabling statute and other regulations for policy arguments, definitions of terms, potential exceptions to the rule, and means of compliance.

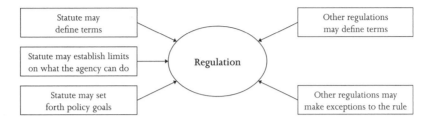

(c) Federal and state regulations are both mandatory authority. As you've discovered (or will discover) in your constitutional law classes, there are areas in which federal law preempts state action. But in areas in which both federal and state governments are authorized to act, it's hard to say that one regulation is more important than the other. Compliance with both is necessary. The penalties for failure to comply with a state regulation may be just as harsh as the penalties for non-compliance with a federal regulation, if not more harsh.

(d) Remember that judicial decisions apply the law to a set of facts. But the holdings of those decisions may establish rules of law that go beyond the facts of a particular decision. Think of the far-reaching effect of *Brown v. Board of Education*. Regulations, on the other hand, are forward-looking requirements that apply across the board to any set of facts that may arise. If the Fifth Circuit opinion is interpreting and applying a regulation to a particular fact situation, its holding is necessarily more narrow than the wide scope of the regulation itself. If, on the other hand, the Fifth Circuit is determining whether a regulation is constitutional or whether it goes beyond the authority of the enabling statute, the Fifth Circuit decision can prevent the agency from enforcing the regulation in any circumstances.

3. A reliable secondary source on disability law — or even a Google search on disability law in employment contexts — would quickly point you to the appropriate statute and regulations and introduce you to the concept of reasonable accommodations in employment. Once you're ready to turn to the primary authorities, you should as always look first to the statute. The Americans with Disabilities Act is codified at 42 U.S.C. §§ 12101-12213; the sections that focus on employment are §§ 12111 through 12117. Section 12111 is titled "Definitions," and that section includes a reference to "reasonable accommodations." Rather than actually defining the term, § 12111 sets forth examples of reasonable accommodations. This is marginally helpful, but it's not as comprehensive a statement of what constitutes a reasonable accommodation as you might like. What now? You've looked at the statute, so now you turn to the regulations promulgated by the Department of Labor.

Title 29 of the Code of Federal Regulations includes Department of Labor regulations; part 1630 of that title includes "Regulations to Implement the Equal Employment Provisions of the Americans with Disabilities Act." Section 1630.2 is titled "Definitions"; paragraph (o) of that regulation defines "reasonable accommodations," and provides additional examples of reasonable accommodations.

The lesson? Even if a statute defines — or at least describes — a term, don't stop there. Regulations often expand on the meaning of terms used in statutes, provide examples of the use of terms, and clarify their application.

4. Here's the original paragraph:

The Internal Revenue Code allows taxpayers to deduct expenses related to a taxpayer's business. There are also regulations enacted by the Internal Revenue Service that provide additional deductions for travel expenses connected to a business. My client claimed a deduction for travel-for-business expenses under the regulation, rather than under the statute.

The Internal Revenue Code is a group of statutes, codified in Title 26 of the U.S. Code. Although it's fine to refer to the Internal Revenue Code (rather than to Title 26 of the U.S. Code) in a letter to the Internal Revenue Service, you should identify which section of the Internal Revenue Code provides for the deduction for business expenses. Moreover, the regulations promulgated by the IRS that address the business expense deduction clarify and provide more information about the deduction; they don't create entirely new deductions not contemplated by the statute. And remember that an agency does not "enact" regulations; rather, it "promulgates" or "adopts" them. In the context of the business expense deduction — one that is established by statute — the taxpayer cannot purport to claim a deduction under the regulation, yet not under the statute. The regulation is, in a sense, subservient to the statute.

The paragraph might be rewritten as follows.

Section 162(a) of the Internal Revenue Code allows a deduction for "ordinary and necessary expenses . . . incurred . . . in carrying on any trade or business." Traveling expenses are expressly included in business expenses in § 162(a)(2). The IRS has promulgated a regulation (26 C.F.R. §1.162-2) to provide more detail about the deduction for travel expenses incurred in a trade or business. My client's claim for a deduction for his business travel expenses is supported by §162 of the Internal Revenue Code and meets the conditions for the business travel deduction set forth in 26 C.F.R. § 1.162.

Ethos, Credibility, and Legal Research

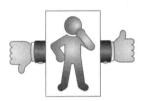

It is the stuff of nightmares for lawyers. You are standing in court and explaining to the judge that a certain precedent, the *Smith* case, requires an outcome for your client. Opposing counsel stands and is recognized. "Your honor, *Smith* was reversed on this issue two months ago," he says. You failed to update the case and you contemplate crawling under the table as the judge turns her inquiring gaze to you.

Or perhaps the judge says, "Counsel, my law clerk tells me you failed to mention the *Jones* case, in which the court explicitly rejected the rule the plaintiff suggests." You are confronted with visions of sanctions for failing to disclose directly adverse authority as required by Model Rule 3.3: Candor Toward the Tribunal. Developing a habit of careful legal research will keep these and other ethical nightmares at bay.

Centuries ago, Aristotle taught that advocates sometimes persuade best through their "ethos" or character. Your reputation as an ethical researcher and your habit of using sources ethically is critically important to becoming an effective attorney. This chapter will introduce you to the rules concerning ethical research, including making sure your sources are still "good law" and that you properly follow the court's rules for citing authorities and filing documents. We examine the importance of building a reputation for credibility through respecting rules and using sources of law ethically, and furthermore, by cultivating a reputation for ethical behavior that goes beyond the rules of professional responsibility.

GLOSSARY

Ethos: The Greek word for "character." Here we use it for Aristotle's idea that the audience's evaluation of an advocate's credibility directly affects the ability of a speaker to persuade.

The ABA Model Rules of Professional Conduct: A set of model rules promulgated by the American Bar Association that jurisdictions adopt to govern lawyers' ethical behavior.

Citator: A system of tracking all the places a source, such as a case or a statute, has been cited by other sources.

Shepard's and Shepardizing: A trademarked name for a system of updating sources to assure the source is still good law by tracking all the places the source has been cited. *Shepard's* is a citator; *"shepardizing"* has become a verb for the process of using a citator to update. Shepard's is part of Lexis.

KeyCite: A trademarked name for a system of updating sources to assure the source is still good law by tracking all of the places the source has been cited. KeyCite is part of Westlaw.

THE MODEL RULES OF PROFESSIONAL CONDUCT AND LEGAL RESEARCH

Each jurisdiction adopts rules that govern the professional conduct of lawyers, almost always based on the American Bar Association's Model Rules of Professional Conduct.[1] The rules set out the minimum boundaries for ethical behavior, but in some contexts you'll want to do more than the rules demand in order to preserve credibility. Regardless, the rules affect legal research in many ways. Here are several rules that apply directly to legal research and using the sources you have found.

Model Rule 1.1:   Competence — This imposes a duty of "competent" representation with the "legal knowledge, skill, thoroughness and preparation reasonably necessary for the representation."[2] The comments to this rule clarify that special training or experience isn't required before taking on a case, but lawyers should consider whether the principles they learned as a part of a general legal education will be enough in the context of a particular

---

1. Or the earlier version, the Model Code of Professional Responsibility.
2. Model R. Prof. Conduct 1.1.

case. Knowing how to find and use the most recent and relevant sources of law is a key part of the general training to which the rule refers.

Model Rule 3.3(a): **Candor Toward The Tribunal** — This states that a lawyer shall not "knowingly" make a false statement of law to a tribunal or "fail to disclose legal authority in the controlling jurisdiction known to the lawyer to be directly adverse to the position of the client and not disclosed by opposing counsel."[3]

This rule imposes several duties on the lawyer. First, lawyers violate the ethical duty when they represent a case as good law, despite the fact that it has been reversed, overruled, or limited in some way. Next, the rule requires the disclosure of relevant adverse authority, if opposing counsel has failed to do so. This assumes that your own research will be thorough enough to find all the mandatory authority that applies to your case, including mandatory authority adverse to your position. Finally, the rule assumes that you will take care in how you represent the content of a case. The Preamble to the Model Rules also imposes a duty of "zealous representation."[4] Often that includes interpreting, analogizing, or distinguishing cases persuasively or in a light favorable to your arguments, in order to help your client. But the Rules make clear that there are limits to how much you can stretch a source when using it.

Model Rule 3.4(c): **Fairness to Opposing Party and Counsel** — This requires lawyers to follow the court's rules. Lawyers may not "knowingly disobey an obligation under the rules of a tribunal."[5] The rule imposes another research duty: to find and follow the local court's rules. These local rules may govern anything from the filing deadlines to the font you use in the brief you submit. Your job will be to find the local court rules that apply, and to follow them.

UPDATING

Ever flees the time; it will wait for no man.
— *Chaucer, Prologue to the Clerk's Tale*

Like time and the tides, the law does not wait, unchanging, for you to find and use it. Let's say today is June 30, 2020. The case you are reading is from 2012, and it quotes a statute that you can see applies to your issue. The case has facts similar to your facts, and you would expect to use both the statute

---

3. Model R. Prof. Conduct 3.3(a).
4. Model R. Prof. Conduct, Preamble and Scope (2).
5. Model R. Prof. Conduct, 3.4(c). The rule lists this exception: "except for an open refusal based on an assertion that no valid obligation exists. . . ."

and the case in your analysis. Good job on research, right? Well, good start. But any problem? Yes . . . in fact it could be a big problem!

The problem is that during the years and days between 2012 and 2020, a legislature or court may have changed the statute, reversed or altered the holding of the case, or a new statute or case may have altered the effect or weight of the source you found. And remember, when you cite a source to the court, you are representing the source is good law. The court needs to be able to rely on your work.

Publishers have developed services for examining other sources that have mentioned your statute or case. These citator services are primarily online now. Currently, few libraries stock the print versions of citators. You must use those mostly electronic services to discover whether your sources still stand, or whether their weight or interpretation has changed in the intervening time. Many researchers also use the services as a finding tool to discover other similar sources, because a case will tend to cite cases or statutes on similar issues. But a citator's most important function is to discover whether a source is still good law. (If you want more help with finding the law, see Appendix A.)

Citators are created by editors scouring other sources for instances in which the original source was used or mentioned. The uses are compiled and sorted. Citator editors have developed systems to let the reader know *how* the new source uses or changes the original source. The scheme of signaling the use (abbreviations in *Shepard's* and colored flags in *KeyCite*) is helpful, but you should never rely on the citator editors' opinions when a signal tells you your source has been changed or diminished in some way. You should *always* read the citing source and form your own opinion as to how the later source affects your source. In addition to being a good research practice, it's your ethical obligation.

COURT RULES

Studying the law means studying rules and how they apply—and we categorize those rules in several ways. For example, one of the ways legal education categorizes rules is whether the rule addresses "substance" or "procedure." This is familiar to even beginning law students. Sometimes you study rules from statutes and cases that are about a category of law that is distinctive because of its substance or content—the law of contracts, the law governing torts, etc. But sometimes you are studying the rules that govern procedures in our justice system. The first-year course devoted to studying the Federal Rules of Civil Procedure is such a "procedure rules" course. The procedural rules govern *how* lawyers do things in court. And what you've seen since you were a child playing board games is true of working in the justice system: the persons who best understand the rules and strategize to use them to their advantage often wins the game.

One part of the advantage of knowing and using the rules to your benefit is that you build credibility by following the rules. Effectively you say to the world, "I am a careful person who pays attention to details. And if I pay attention to details, you can imagine that I am even more careful about my analysis and how I use the law." But beyond the advantage you gain in credibility and the ability to formulate a winning strategy, you also have an ethical duty to follow a court's rules according to Model Rule 3.4(c): Fairness to Opposing Party and Counsel. To meet that obligation, you must know that each court has its own rules, and you must know how to find and follow them. A court's rules are primary authority.

Sometimes court rules will be large compilations governing procedures in many different courts in a jurisdiction. For example, the Federal Rules of Civil Procedure govern procedure in all federal courts. Or the Federal Rules of Appellate Procedure govern procedure in all the federal appellate courts — the federal circuit courts and the United States Supreme Court. Similarly, individual states will compile rules that apply in many courts within the jurisdiction. Usually these compilations of court rules are published as a part of the statutory code (although court rules are, of course, not statutes and have no relationship to the legislature).

Other times you will be looking for the "local rules," the rules promulgated by individual courts that govern details of procedure not addressed in the larger compilations. These local rules will expand upon and not replace the larger compilations of rules mentioned above. Local rules may govern anything from how and where to file a document to the font you must use in documents submitted to a particular court. Look for local rules on the courts' websites, or contact the clerks of the courts to find out how to obtain a copy.

In addition to other court rules, as a part of your ethical duty you will follow the citation rules the local court requires. These rules may instruct you to follow a certain citation manual or guide. Or they may impose other requirements for how to cite in documents addressed to the court. This is also a fairness issue because the citation rules ensure that both the court and opposing counsel can find the sources to which you refer. For more about citation, see Appendix B.

You will find times when the rules themselves are at issue. Rules are at issue most often when they are part of the big compilations of rules for a jurisdiction that seek to ensure fairness within the system. The local rules that indicate a particular judge's preferences for font choice or who in chambers receives and logs-in documents are less likely to be challenged. When the issues involve fairness and rules, the analysis may be complex and require all your skills as a researcher working with rules and cases interpreting rules. You will follow the same procedures you would for any other legal issue — finding mandatory precedent addressing the issue and then moving to persuasive authority if you need it to make effective arguments.

WRITING ETHICALLY: USING SOURCES TO PROMOTE CREDIBILITY

One of the several requirements of Model Rule 3.3: Candor Toward the Tribunal is the expectation that you will ethically use the sources you find. Sometimes a use is clearly out-of-bounds — like misrepresentation. Other times, you will need to decide for yourself how far you are willing to stretch or narrow a holding to make it work for your client. Always remember that in addition to serving the present client, you want to keep your reputation with the court intact for the next client and the next time you appear before a court. As you write using the sources you've found, here are some points to remember about the ethical use of sources:

1. *Misrepresenting a source by leaving out key information does more than destroy credibility; it is a violation of the rules.* Don't cruise through a case looking for any phrase that might help you regardless of the intent of the court. Don't trim a quote just to serve your purposes at the expense of giving the reader an impression that is inconsistent with reading the whole case. For example, in *Precision Specialty Metals, Inc. v. U.S.,*[6] a court ordered an attorney to file a motion "forthwith." The attorney filed the motion twelve days later and the court struck it from the record. On appeal, the attorney claimed the sources she cited defined "forthwith" as "with reasonable dispatch." She omitted the parts of the cases that defined "forthwith" as "immediately" and "usually within 24 hours." The court imposed sanctions on the attorney.

2. *If mandatory authority seems apparently to favor the other side, you must address it.* In most cases, you'll address all the mandatory authority that applies directly to your case. If lots of case law directly applies, you may decide to address the cases that are most similar or most typical. Ignoring a case that is directly applicable, but is better for the other side, is not an option. It's important to address it for two reasons: First, you are obligated to disclose it to the court under Model Rule 3.3 (a). You may not assume that because the case favors the other side, the other party will address it and you can ignore it. But beyond the ethical duty to disclose adverse authority, you want to be able to affect how the court sees that case by framing it your way. Most likely you can distinguish the facts of your case from the facts of the precedent. Or perhaps you can suggest that the rationale of the case should be read narrowly, or that the policy the court identifies in precedent doesn't apply here. But you certainly want to affect the way the court reads that case, and not leave it to the other side to characterize the case. Ignoring it is not a good option.

---

6. 315 F.3d 1346 (Fed. Cir. 2003).

3. *When researching online, to protect your own credibility, evaluate the credibility of the sources you find.* You should always question the validity and durability of the sources you find online or in print. Some of the questions you must ask as you evaluate online sources include questions about the credibility of the author (Who wrote it? Who sponsors the site? What are their credentials? Do they have a stake in the material that might build in biases?), as well as questions about the accuracy of the content (Can you verify the information elsewhere? Is it complete? How often is the site updated? Did the site have permission to use what it cited?). Much of the time, you will be researching primary sources and finding the sources in highly reputable sites — government sites, commercial sites like Bloomberg, Lexis, or Westlaw, or sites like Google Scholar that harvest sources from government sites. But when you venture from the well-documented sites, to preserve your credibility, you must evaluate the sites where you find sources.

4. *Although holdings are elastic and can be framed in ways that benefit either side, make considered decisions about how far you are willing to go when representing what a court said.* As we noted above, you may not misrepresent the law. Nor would a good lawyer fail to frame a case persuasively for a client. There is a gray area between misrepresentation and failing to frame the law persuasively. There isn't one right answer when you are interpreting language. It's what makes lawyers' jobs interesting and creative. But you will need to develop a sense about how far you are willing to go, based on your own comfort level. That "comfort level" gauge is your conscience and your sense that you need to preserve credibility. Make sure others can at least see what you saw when you wrote persuasively about a case. Think about how far you want to go.

5. *Build credibility by carefully choosing language that precisely reflects what you take from the case.* You can do this in several ways. One is to carefully reflect the procedural posture of the case. For example, if the appellate court is reviewing a motion for summary judgment, the court may decide to *remand* the case — send it back to the trial court with instructions about what to do next. The summary judgment standard is complicated, and you'll learn more about it in your Civil Procedure class. But the language you choose should reflect that the appellate court found that a trial court taking up the case on remand could possibly determine a particular outcome — not that the appellate court held that the outcome was correct.

    Similarly, don't represent everything in a case as "the court held. . . ." If the language you want to use from the case is dicta and not necessary to the holding, you will not say that the court "held," but rather that the court "stated" or "noted." This careful word choice will build your credibility.

EXAMPLES AND EXPLANATIONS

Examples

It's always good to get some hands-on experience. Here are some questions that will allow you to practice researching ethically. Law is open-ended, changing as time passes. And the tools to find law are open-ended, changing often just like the law. Thus, the questions below are open-ended so that you can strike out on your own path without needing to replicate someone else's out-of-date research. Take our questions as a starting point and see where you go. The Explanations discuss some of the things you may see on your research path. Remember that if you need help knowing how to use various tools to search, look to Appendix A.

1. Find a case from one of your casebooks that is at least forty years old. First use Shepard's on Lexis to update it. Then use KeyCite on Westlaw to update it. Your research professor may ask you to bring the results to class so you can discuss what you found with other students who updated other cases. Find the answers to these questions:

   a. Is your case still good law? Has it been reversed, overruled, or superseded?
   b. Find a case that "distinguished" your case. How do you know in Shepard's that the new case has been distinguished from your case? How do you know in KeyCite?
   c. Find a case that followed your case. What is the symbol in Shepard's? What is the symbol in KeyCite?
   d. Are the results in both KeyCite and Shepard's the same?
   e. Choose a symbol like 'followed,' 'distinguished,' or 'reversed' in Shepard's. Read the case with the symbol. Do you agree with the way the editors used the symbol?
   f. Choose a case with a yellow flag in KeyCite. Does a yellow flag mean you cannot use the case anymore?
   g. What is the effect of a case being reversed? Overruled? Superseded?

2. Find the court rules for a trial court in your jurisdiction. Answer the following questions:

   a. Do the rules address how holidays, Saturdays, and Sundays are treated by the court?
   b. Is there a dress code for this court?
   c. Are there rules that govern how lawyers respond to discovery requests?
   d. Where do you file a motion?

3. Find the Federal Rules of Appellate Practice online. Answer these questions:

   a. Which rule governs writing briefs?
   b. Can you find a rule that describes the contents of a jurisdictional statement? Is it the same for the appellant and the appellee?
   c. Which rule explains the requirements for writing an appendix to the brief?

Explanations

1. Your case may or may not provide answers for all of these questions, but if you don't get much experience using the first case you choose, try another. You'll also gain experience if you stop to update the cases and statutes you use in your legal writing assignments. It will give you a chance to see how updating can be a finding tool for more cases or statutes that may apply to your issue. You may need to update again right before you submit a document to a court (or to your teacher who will grade your paper!).

   a. Remember that each service may develop different ways of communicating whether the source is still good law as time passes. As this book went to press, Shepard's uses icons online and KeyCite has a flags system. The other important point to remember is that you should read the sources to make sure you agree with the assessment of the service editor. You may see that a case has been reversed or see a red flag or stop sign, but upon reading the case, you find that, although a part of the case was reversed, the part you need for your issue is still good law.
   b. This question just wants you to get your "hands dirty" and to see how the signals work in both of the most popular citators.
   c. Same as above. You want to get used to checking both what the symbols mean and whether you agree with the assessment.
   d. The results may be the same, but often they are different. Citators are services from publishing companies, and they are most similar to a secondary source and are not "the law." Because the editorial practices may be different in different companies, the citators' results may not be exactly the same. Both should list the sources citing your source, but they may characterize the sources in slightly different ways.
   e. Remember that when the results of updating change the way you use your source, you must read what the editors read and come to your own conclusions about how subsequent sources affect your source.
   f. As we go to press, KeyCite uses yellow flags in instances that should not bother the researcher with the validity of the source. For example, if a case mentions your source but notes that your source was about a

completely different issue, you will see a yellow flag. It does not affect the value of your case.

g. If a case is overruled, it is no longer good precedent and you should not use it. If a case is reversed, it is sent back to the lower court to decide it again. It may involve denial of summary judgment, or a new rule. You'll need to read the reversing case carefully to discern its effect. If a case or statute is superseded, the case or statute no longer carries mandatory or persuasive authority.

2. Again, answers will vary. We tried to supply questions that most trial court local rules will address. Our goal here is for you to find and interact with local rules, not for you to find a specific answer. If your local rules did not contain answers and you are curious, you can try another jurisdiction. Or you might want the experience of calling the clerk of the court to ask a question.

   a. Only some of the local rules we examined expressly addressed Saturdays and Sundays. Many addressed how holidays would be treated.
   b. Local rules often address either decorum or a dress code or both. Most often rules required "dignity" in both dress and actions within the court. Sometimes rules addressed situations like sitting on railings or tilting back in a chair.
   c. Rules governing discovery are very common in local rules. Sometimes the rules set a time limit; other times the rules explain how various discovery documents will be treated by the court.

3. Again, we realize that it is possible for the rules to change before you work with this book. In fact, amendments to the Federal Rules of Appellate Procedure take effect in December 2016. It is unlikely the answers to the questions you are exploring will change, but be aware that they might.

   a. Currently Rule 28 of the Federal Rules of Appellate Procedure governs briefs.
   b. The appellant's brief contains a jurisdictional statement that includes the following: the basis for the district court's or agency's subject-matter jurisdiction, with citations to applicable statutory provisions and stating relevant facts establishing jurisdiction; the basis for the court of appeals' jurisdiction, with citations to applicable statutory provisions and stating relevant facts establishing jurisdiction; the filing dates establishing the timeliness of the appeal or petition for review; and an assertion that the appeal is from a final order or judgment that disposes of all parties' claims, or information establishing the court of appeals' jurisdiction on some other basis. FRAP 28 (a)(4). The appellee needs only to include a jurisdiction statement if the appellee is dissatisfied with the appellant's statement. FRAP 28 (b)(1).
   c. FRAP 30.

CHAPTER 10

Secondary Sources

Everyone eats. Sometimes we eat plain, unadulterated food — broccoli, steak, rice, baked potatoes, bananas — that's good for us and that provides whatever nutrients we need. We may or may not always like those unadulterated foods (given the choices before us), but what they provide is essential. What we might in our secret heart of hearts prefer are processed and complex foods — from chicken fried steak and Frito pie to beef bourguignon and *huevos rancheros*. If we think of primary authorities as the broccoli and bananas of sources — you must eat or use those to thrive — secondary authorities correlate, in the food world, to M&Ms, pizza, eggs benedict, and eggplant parmesan. The variety is enormous; the flavors can be complex or simple; we eat these wildly different foods in very different contexts; and all of these complex and processed foods depend upon the broccoli, eggs, milk, and bananas of the food world.

The analogy goes on. We might not want to admit to anyone that we eat Cheetos, but that doesn't make them any less tasty. So it goes for secondary authorities. We would rarely, if at all, cite to some secondary authorities in a brief or other document, but that doesn't mean that those authorities aren't useful in their own way. There are foods that we eat on the run — we don't have time to linger — and so there are secondary authorities that provide us with quick and dirty introductions to what we need to know. On the other hand, sometimes secondary authorities may be like the pleasures of a multi-course meal in a fine (and expensive!) restaurant. Our appreciation of the food is

Menu

(OF SECONDARY AUTHORITIES)

Appetizers
American Law Reports
Legal Encyclopedias

Main Courses
Treatises
Law Review Articles

Sides
Study Guides

Desserts
Blogs

123

heightened when we know all of the work and expertise that went into its preparation. And, the company with whom we share a sit-down meal adds to its enjoyment. Some secondary authorities deepen our understanding of the law; they bring new insights and perspectives. Those authorities reflect the research and in-depth analysis undertaken by experts in the field — practitioners and scholars alike — and, if used properly, can strengthen an argument or help an attorney find the best way to further her client's interests.

Eating cotton candy at home just seems wrong. It's not made for that kind of ordinary, everyday consumption. And some secondary sources — be they practitioner-oriented treatises on esoteric topics, legal encyclopedias that very briefly summarize complex topics, or study guides aimed at first-year law students — are like that too. They're designed for use in specific contexts; citing or referring to those sources outside of those contexts shows a misunderstanding of their purposes and will likely reflect poorly on you as an attorney (or as a law student).

There are too many different kinds of secondary authorities to describe in this chapter. Instead, we will help you identify and evaluate secondary sources so that you know in what contexts a particular kind of secondary source might be helpful and how best to use that authority. We'll describe some of the most frequently used secondary authorities and give you tips on how to figure out the relative usefulness of secondary authorities more generally.

GLOSSARY

American Law Reports: A series of articles (sometimes accompanied by the text of a court decision), published in the style of a reporter, that describe specific points of law. Typical titles of American Law Reports (ALR) articles include "Liability for Injuries Caused by Cat," "Expectation of Privacy in and Discovery of Social Networking Web Site Postings and Communications," and "Validity and Construction of Statutes, Ordinances, or Regulations Concerning the Sale of Horse Meat for Human Consumption." A typical ALR entry consists of an article that introduces an issue of law (primarily narrow common law issues) and then gathers and summarizes leading cases from all U.S. jurisdictions that address that issue. The ALR entry also provides citations to other secondary sources that discuss the issue. An ALR article is a good way to get an in-depth summary of the state of the law on a narrow issue and to find relevant primary authorities across jurisdictions. ALR articles are typically not cited in documents filed with a court or in law-related scholarship. If you can find an ALR article on your topic, it can save time and energy as the article will point you directly to relevant primary authorities on specific points of law.

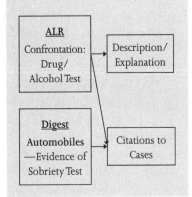

Connections: ALRs and digests point you to cases on particular topics. If you need an explanation of the legal issue, find a relevant ALR entry and then read the description. If you want to go straight to the cases, use the digests.

Black letter law: Summaries of common law principles that are informally accepted as being true across jurisdictions. Lawyers and first-year law students alike know that, in order to be enforceable, a contract must involve both an offer and an acceptance of that offer. That statement of black letter law is easy to remember and true, whether you're a law student in North Dakota or a lawyer in Maine. What statements of black letter law fail to capture are all the nuances and complexities of the common law. There's no book that states all the black letter law, and you can't cite black letter law (because there's nothing to cite). Restatements (described on page 126) are probably the closest thing we have to a collection of black letter law statements. Legal encyclopedias, student study guides, and Bar review materials often include statements of black letter law.

Digests: Indexes to cases. Imagine that you are looking for a case and have no access to the Internet, no smart phone, no technology. How will you find a court decision that addresses a particular point of law? Remember, people did practice law before the Internet. A digest, usually published as a series of volumes, organizes cases by the legal topics that they discuss. A digest is a finding tool; in our food analogy, a digest is like a spoon or a fork — it gets you to the authorities and allows you to use them. Digests are published in print and organize the law into a hierarchy of topics. Once you find the topic that interests you, you'll find in the digest short summaries of cases that address that topic. Digests don't explain or analyze primary authority; they simply identify cases that discuss particular points of law. West's Key Number System on Westlaw is an online corollary to print digests. Find a topic in the Key Number System and you'll find cases that address that topic from every jurisdiction.

Formbooks: Single volumes or multi-volume sets that provide model forms for attorneys to use in litigation and transactional work. Those forms are generic and must *always* be revised to reflect a client's particular situation and needs. A formbook for use in a litigation practice would include forms for motions, affidavits, depositions, and settlement agreements. Forms for employment agreements,

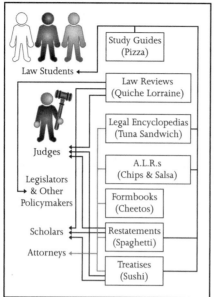

articles of incorporation, partnership agreements, wills, liens, and deeds of trust would appear in a formbook designed for a transactions practice.

Law Reviews and Journals: Regularly published journals — usually published by U.S. law schools — that collect scholarship authored by law faculty, law students, and, less frequently, judges and practitioners. Law review articles are often very long, with lots of footnotes, and address issues that are of current interest, argue for law reform, or analyze a problem from a new and usually high-level perspective. These secondary sources are for sophisticated readers — they are usually directed to other academics, judges, and policy-makers — and can be used to make policy arguments and to support a particular interpretation of the law.

Legal Dictionaries: A dictionary of law-related terms arranged in alphabetical order. Legal dictionaries define terms and words used in law contexts and briefly describe their usage, both in current contexts and historical ones. Citations to cases that illustrate the use of the terms and words may be included in a legal dictionary's definition. Legal dictionaries are infrequently cited in court or scholarly documents. *Black's Law Dictionary* is probably the most widely recognized legal dictionary.

Legal Encyclopedias: An encyclopedia of law-related terms and doctrines arranged in alphabetical order. Legal encyclopedias provide quick introductions to legal topics and often some citations to leading (although often old) cases and other authorities that discuss those topics. Entries in legal encyclopedias are usually a few paragraphs long. The citations to other authorities are not nearly as comprehensive as the citations included in ALRs and digests. The two leading legal encyclopedias are *Corpus Juris Secundum* and *American Jurisprudence*. Never cite a legal encyclopedia to support a statement of law. They encapsulate legal doctrines in easily digestible bites, but do not provide in-depth analysis.

Restatements: A series of statements of the common law (and in some cases, statutes as well) on many different topics, published by the American Law Institute ("ALI"). Members of the ALI are experts in their fields — scholars, judges, and practitioners — who formulate statements of accepted common law principles and analyze differences in those principles across jurisdictions. Because their authors are so well-recognized and because each proposed Restatement is rigorously reviewed and vetted by committees within and the membership of the ALI, the Restatements are often cited in documents addressed to courts and in legal scholarship. Restatements "state" the common law in a code-like format and include comments, notes, and citations to cases in jurisdictions around the country.

Study Guides: Texts designed for law students that correspond to law school courses and summarize a particular area of law. Required texts for law school courses usually consist of case after case after case (with sometimes a statute or other authority thrown in for good measure). Study guides, usually written by law school professors, summarize and compare the holdings of cases and other authorities, and help law students make sense of authorities covered in class. You would *never* cite a study guide.

Treatises: Sometimes single-volume, sometimes many-volume texts that discuss and analyze an area of law. Treatises have many audiences: some are directed at law students; some at practitioners; and still others at scholars. Treatises are usually authored by well-recognized experts in the field and provide a sophisticated discussion and analysis of a topic. Treatises (at least those treatises that are intended for scholars and practitioners) are sometimes cited in briefs and other court documents and in scholarship. Practice guides are a particular type of treatise; they focus on a practice area (e.g., bankruptcy, insurance law, patents) and provide in-depth description and analysis of the law in that area, guidance for lawyers who practice in that area, and often forms and related documents that are frequently used by practitioners.

THE BASICS YOU NEED TO KNOW

It's often useful to start your research in a secondary source.

- Some secondary sources provide quick introductions to either an area of law or a particular doctrine or rule. The quicker the introduction, the less likely that you would cite the secondary source.
- Secondary sources can introduce students and attorneys to terms of art used in particular practice contexts. Knowing the language and terms used in an area will help you craft better searches in whatever online resources — like Google, Lexis, or FastCase — you might use.
- The leading primary authorities on a particular topic are often cited in secondary sources. Again, knowing those authorities will help you find other related and relevant primary authorities.

Some secondary sources should be used only to inform and educate.

- Study guides and other secondary sources that are short on citations to primary authorities should never be cited in scholarship or documents submitted to a court.
- The usefulness of secondary sources like study guides and the descriptive texts in ALRs lies in their summary of primary authorities and their description of a particular topic or doctrine. There would be no reason to cite such a summary of law in any document filed with a court (instead, you would cite to primary authority that supports your position) or in a research paper for your law school classes.

Some secondary sources should be used only as pointers to primary authorities and to more sophisticated secondary authorities.

- Digests and their online corollaries, the Key Number System on Westlaw and the LexisNexis Topic Index and Headnotes, gather cases from all U.S. jurisdictions that address particular points of law. Using a digest as opposed to a keyword search can sometimes lead to more relevant cases and sources, or to cases and sources that would not have been discovered at all by means of a keyword search.

Connections: A keyword search for "same sex marriage" will retrieve only those documents that include the words "same," "sex," and "marriage." Those search results would likely *not* include documents that described same sex marriage in other terms, like, for example, "gay marriage" (although some keyword searches include searches for synonyms). But a digest categorizes and indexes cases on the basis of the actual concepts they discuss, rather than the particular words used in the opinion. A LexisNexis Headnote, under the topic of "Equal Protection," includes cases collected under the heading "Gender & Sex," no matter what terms (e.g., gay, lesbian, transgender, homosexual, same sex) the court uses to describe gender and sex. Westlaw Key Number 54(2) in the "Marriage" category similarly collects cases relating to same-sex and other non-traditional unions, however those unions might be described by courts.

Never take any form for granted, and never, ever use a form without carefully reviewing and revising it to fit your own circumstances.

- Think of a form in a formbook as the lowest common denominator (if you remember your elementary school math). Forms by definition are designed to serve in as many relevant contexts as possible, and so, much of the language in forms is generic and not specific.
- Forms should *never* be copied verbatim. First, the terms of the transaction or activity that the form applies to must be carefully described. Second, every jurisdiction's laws are different. A provision in a form that has a particular consequence in one jurisdiction might have a very different consequence in another jurisdiction. In a litigation context, a form may not comply with the court's local rules and orders. Any form must be adapted and revised to take into account the law and custom of the applicable jurisdiction.

A secondary source is stronger (i.e., it can be used to support an argument or to provide guidance) to the extent that it cites many primary authorities.

- If a secondary source cites lots of primary authorities, it inspires confidence. It shows that the author has carefully and thoroughly researched the topic and that she can support the statements or arguments she makes. Law review articles include many, many citations to primary authorities and well-recognized secondary authorities.

Always carefully consider the author of a secondary source.

- To the extent that the author is a recognized expert in the field — either a scholar or a practitioner — it's more appropriate to cite the secondary source in scholarship or in documents filed in court.
- If a secondary source has no individual author (for example, a legal encyclopedia), it's not something that you would ordinarily cite. Again, the source might still be useful for your research, but without an author, it's hard for a court or anyone else to evaluate its reliability as the source of expert knowledge or commentary.

Think about the audience and the purpose of the secondary source before you rely too heavily on it.

- As a law student you shouldn't rely on materials written for the lay public. Those sources have a very different focus from texts directed to lawyers and law students. They may oversimplify legal doctrine and may simply be wrong. Sources written for lawyers and law students are likely to approach problems in a way that corresponds to the legal analysis you are learning in law school.

If you are researching a topic that is very current, make sure that you choose a secondary source that is equally current.

- If your research question centers on the enforceability of online adhesion contracts, a classic treatise on contracts written in the 1990s may be of some use. That treatise would likely describe the requirements of contract formation in the context of standard form consumer contracts. But even the most reliable and well-recognized secondary source from the 1990s will not address the ubiquitous shrink-wrap online license. You will need to find a recently updated treatise that cites cases and other authorities that consider the enforceability of online adhesion contracts.

Consider the publisher or the source of the secondary authority.

- The Internet is full of secondary sources, some of which are reliable, others of which are woefully unhelpful and, in fact, dangerous to rely upon. Consider the reputation of the publisher or poster of the information. Does a website include enough information about the publisher and author so that you can evaluate their expertise? If not, steer clear of that source. Is the individual or group publishing or posting the information advocating a particular position? If that's the case, take that into account when you consider the reliability of the information.

- As a general rule, evaluate a secondary source as you would any information. Does it come from an author and publisher that are recognized authorities? Is it updated frequently to reflect new primary authority? Is it intended for an audience that is relatively sophisticated and knowledgeable about the law? Does it support its statements with citations to primary authority? Only if you answer yes to those questions is it an authority that you should trust.

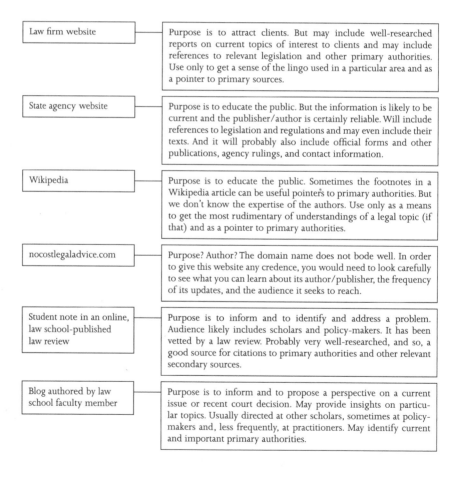

| Law firm website | Purpose is to attract clients. But may include well-researched reports on current topics of interest to clients and may include references to relevant legislation and other primary authorities. Use only to get a sense of the lingo used in a particular area and as a pointer to primary sources. |

| State agency website | Purpose is to educate the public. But the information is likely to be current and the publisher/author is certainly reliable. Will include references to legislation and regulations and may even include their texts. And it will probably also include official forms and other publications, agency rulings, and contact information. |

| Wikipedia | Purpose is to educate the public. Sometimes the footnotes in a Wikipedia article can be useful pointers to primary authorities. But we don't know the expertise of the authors. Use only as a means to get the most rudimentary of understandings of a legal topic (if that) and as a pointer to primary authorities. |

| nocostlegaladvice.com | Purpose? Author? The domain name does not bode well. In order to give this website any credence, you would need to look carefully to see what you can learn about its author/publisher, the frequency of its updates, and the audience it seeks to reach. |

| Student note in an online, law school-published law review | Purpose is to inform and to identify and address a problem. Audience likely includes scholars and policy-makers. It has been vetted by a law review. Probably very well-researched, and so, a good source for citations to primary authorities and other relevant secondary sources. |

| Blog authored by law school faculty member | Purpose is to inform and to propose a perspective on a current issue or recent court decision. May provide insights on particular topics. Usually directed at other scholars, sometimes at policy-makers and, less frequently, at practitioners. May identify current and important primary authorities. |

HOW IT WORKS: AN EXAMPLE

Suppose your clients' landlord has given your clients an eviction notice. Those clients, an unmarried couple who have resided in the apartment on a month-to-month lease for two years, practice a religion whose values differ greatly from those of their landlord. While the notice fails to state the reasons behind the eviction, the landlord has told the tenants that she objects both to their unmarried status and to their religion.

You know little about landlord-tenant law. So far, you've reviewed the lease and determined that its terms allow the landlord to terminate the lease for any reason. Your problem now is to determine whether your clients have a good argument to prevent the eviction.

You wonder (among many things) whether this effort to evict your clients might violate the federal Fair Housing Act. But you know nothing about the Fair Housing Act (other than its name). What are some secondary sources that might be useful and what should you expect to find in each of them?

There are lots of free online resources that provide information about federal fair housing laws. Non-profit civil rights organizations describe the laws and provide data about housing, Wikipedia includes an article on the Fair Housing Act, and other free non-government sites purport to define fair housing or summarize federal and state fair housing laws. But probably the best resource that, thankfully, appears at the top of any search engine's results list is the website maintained by the U.S. Department of Housing and Urban Development that focuses on fair housing laws and executive orders. That website lists all the federal statutes — not just the Fair Housing Act — that relate to potential discrimination in housing and describes the types of discrimination each statute prohibits. Once you've reviewed that website's description of the relevant federal statutes, you will at least have your bearings. You can then explore that site further to find federal regulations, guidance in filing discrimination claims, and lists of cases involving discrimination claims in housing. You could use other free non-government websites — perhaps some sponsored by well-recognized advocacy groups — to discover approaches and arguments that might help your clients. There is so much free and reliable information online about fair housing law that there would be no need to consult websites like Wikipedia.

Google Scholar, another free online resource, might point you to law review articles, as well as some cases and even books that discuss fair housing law and policy. The full text of the law review articles and books may or may not be freely available online; if not, you will need to find the law review articles in a commercial resource like Lexis, Westlaw, Bloomberg Law, or Hein Online, and you might visit your law library to find the books. Law review articles and books are likely to discuss fair housing policies, potential improvements to the laws, and important cases that have interpreted those laws. What they're less likely to include are instructions and guidance on protecting individual rights to fair housing and strategies that an attorney might employ to ensure that his clients realize the benefits of those statutes.

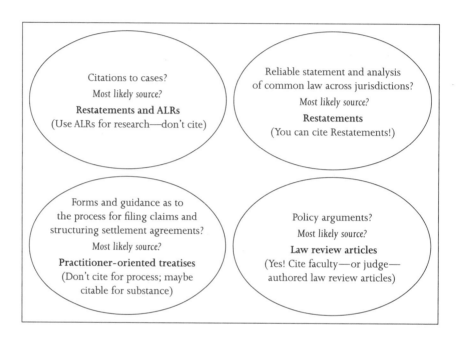

In addition to including the full text of law review articles, commercial resources like Bloomberg Law, Lexis, and Westlaw also include secondary sources directed at practitioners that provide detailed information on fair housing laws and their enforcement. For example, on Westlaw, the treatise titled "Housing Discrimination Law and Litigation" describes what must be proven in order to allege a violation of the Fair Housing Act, to what extent family status may be the basis of an eviction, who has standing to sue, and which defendants may be liable. That treatise also describes the procedures for filing a claim with the Department of Housing and Urban Development, what claims for damages may be litigated in court, and whether attorneys' fees may be recovered by plaintiffs in an action to enforce federal fair housing laws.

The Restatements are also available on commercial resources like Westlaw and Lexis. The portion of the Restatement of Property that covers landlord-tenant relationships might be helpful. It's possible that state law would provide additional protections to your clients. In addition to stating well-accepted principles of landlord-tenant common law, the Restatement of Property would include citations to leading cases (with luck, in your jurisdiction) that might suggest additional grounds to fight the eviction.

For a synopsis of the Fair Housing Act, insofar as it protects against discrimination on the basis of marital and family status, as well as cases that interpret it, you might look to ALRs. For example, the ALR entry titled "Refusal to Rent based on Sex or Familial Status as Violation of Fair Housing Act" might lead you to cases similar to that of your client. While neither the Restatement nor an ALR entry would provide the kind of practical guidance that a practitioner-oriented secondary source would, they can save you time in your research by helping you identify relevant authorities and summarizing case law.

WRITING ABOUT SECONDARY AUTHORITIES

1. *Don't cite a secondary source as a statement of law.* When writing law school papers, briefs and other documents filed in court, and memoranda to colleagues in a firm, always cite primary sources when describing what the law is. Never cite a secondary source as if it were a primary authority, and never cite a secondary source when describing the holding of a case or the requirements of a statute.

2. *Secondary sources can be cited to show agreement — or conflict — across jurisdictions.* Sometimes a seminar paper or a court document calls for a summary of case law across jurisdictions. For example, a lawyer might want to make an argument that the resolution of a question of first impression in a particular state's courts should mirror the resolution of that question in the vast majority of jurisdictions across the country. To support that argument, the attorney might cite a Restatement, which would state the principle of law that is well-accepted across the country, analyze the issue, and provide citations to primary authorities.

3. *A secondary authority can be used to support an argument as to what the law should be.* If an issue is particularly controversial and unsettled, a well-reasoned policy argument suggested by an expert in the field can be very persuasive. Law review articles — especially those authored by scholars in a particular field or judges who have special expertise in an area — are excellent sources for policy arguments.

4. *Don't write about secondary authorities. Use them to support an argument or a claim.* In law school and other scholarly papers, references to secondary sources should usually appear in footnotes. For example, the text of a paper might state that commentators support a particular interpretation of a statute, and then go on to describe that interpretation. Footnotes that support that statement would cite the secondary source and perhaps include a quote from the secondary source, or briefly describe the argument made in the secondary source.

5. *Distinguish between secondary sources that (i) summarize and help the reader understand an area of law and make her research more efficient; and (ii) secondary sources that add substance to an area of law.* While you would never cite the first category of sources (the tools — e.g., legal dictionaries and ALRs), you might cite sources in the second category, as they (like law review articles, restatements, and some treatises) add something new to the discussion of primary authorities.

EXAMPLES AND EXPLANATIONS

Examples

I. The partner in your firm has mumbled something to you about a problem involving "interlocking directors" (in her words) in two companies that might compete against each other. That's all she said and she expects to receive a memo on the topic next week. You know absolutely nothing about interlocking directors.

1. You start by Googling "interlocking directors" and find the following information. Which of these online resources might be useful, and how might each of them be used, if at all, in the research process?

   a. A Wikipedia article titled "Interlocking Directorate."

   b. A definition of "interlocking directorate" on businessdictionary .com (a website with lots of banners advertising investment services).

   c. A series of blog posts on the Harvard Law School Forum on Corporate Governance and Financial Regulation website that describe recent scholarship and new federal regulations on interlocking boards.

   d. A report titled "Interlocking Directorates: A Sleeping Bear Awakens?" on the website of a well-recognized, global insurance provider.

   e. A 2012 article in Forbes titled "Why Should We Care About Corporate Interlocks?"

   f. A report on the website of a large and well-known (for good lawyering) law firm titled "The Clayton Act and Interlocking Directors — New Legislative and Regulatory Developments."

2. Having gotten your bearings on what interlocking directors are and why it might be a problem if the firm's client served on the board of directors of two competing corporations, you now want to better understand the relevant statute, identify cases that interpret it, and

determine how to counsel the firm's client as to his service on the boards of competing corporations.

Consider the following statements and approaches. Are these statements true and do they suggest good approaches for the researcher?

a. A good way to start and to find all of the cases on the topic would be to enter the term "interlocking directors" in the search box of a commercial research database like Lexis or Westlaw.

b. Finding the relevant statute in a commercial research database is likely to lead you to cases that construe the statute.

c. Starting with the Restatements is a good idea, as they bring together case law from all jurisdictions.

d. Practitioner-oriented treatises on antitrust law would be helpful as you think about how to counsel your client. Starting your research here would be most efficient.

e. Law reviews will help you quickly identify relevant case law and can be cited to demonstrate what case law holds.

II. Your client claims that she suffered emotional injury when, while riding on a ski lift, she saw the chair in front of her fall to the ground shortly before its occupants were to get off the lift. Although your client was not physically injured, she was very close to the event and escaped injury only as a result of the quick thinking of the ski lift operators. The question of whether an individual can recover for negligent inflic- tion of emotional distress where there was no physical injury is an open one in your jurisdiction. The lower court held against your client and you have appealed to the state's intermediate court.

In researching and then making your argument to the appellate court, how might the following secondary sources be useful to you?

1. Restatement of the Law of Torts
2. ALR
3. A legal encyclopedia such as *American Jurisprudence*
4. Law review articles
5. Treatises on torts
6. Digests and the key number system in Westlaw or topic headnotes in Lexis

III. Consider the following sentences. Are the secondary sources used appropriately?

1. Rule 506(b) in the C.F.R. allows a company to raise as much capital as it can, provided that no more than thirty-five of the people buying shares are unaccredited as defined in the Securities Act of 1933. S. Teemed Faculty Member, *The Ins and Outs of Small Business Funding: Rule 506 and the Securities Act of 1933*, 101 HARV. L. REV 2467 (2014).

2. Although most states follow the "best interests of the child rule" in determining custody decisions, not all states do. "In divorce proceedings, the 'best interests' of the child is a proper and feasible criterion for making a decision as to which of the two parents will be accorded custody of the child." 24A Am. Jur. 2d Divorce and Separation § 849. For example, both Tennessee and North Dakota statutes set forth a number of criteria that courts must consider, many of which have nothing to do with the best interests of the child. A. Noted Judge, *A Fifty State Survey of Child Custody Statutes*, 39 Calif. L. Rev. 537 (2015). Many have argued for a more inclusive, holistic rule that accounts for the circumstances of parents, siblings, and each of their rights. Lon G. Thyme Scholar, *Looking Ahead: A Better Approach to Child Custody Determinations*, 48 Ala. L. Rev. 29 (2011).

3. It is well-settled law that a contract may be voided if one of its parties was intoxicated at the time the party entered into the contract and the other party had reason to know that the intoxicated party was unable to understand his or her responsibilities under the contract. Restatement (Second) of Contracts § 16 Intoxicated Persons (1981).

Explanations

I.1. a. The Wikipedia article would be useful only to get a very general idea of what the term "interlocking directors" refers to. If you're lucky, a Wikipedia article may include footnotes to the Clayton Act, the federal antitrust statute that sometimes prohibits interlocking directors among competing companies. If the Wikipedia article did not cite the statute, it would be of little use at all.

b. A website like businessdictionary.com usually provides little or no information about the persons who author the information on the website or other sources of the information. You should be very skeptical about relying on any of the information on this kind of commercial website.

c. Blog posts on the Harvard Law School Forum on Corporate Governance and Financial Regulation website are likely to be authored by Harvard faculty or other scholars with significant expertise on the subject. That said, these blog postings are unlikely to be of too much use to you early in the research process. They are likely written for experts and others with at least some knowledge of the antitrust and corporate governance landscape. Once you become well-versed in the issues raised by interlocking directors, you may well want to revisit this site. And if you found information there that was helpful, and its author was identified as a faculty member or other scholar, citing that website to support an interpretation or argument would be perfectly acceptable.

d. Information on the website of a commercial entity is likely to reflect the interests of that entity and is likely to be addressed to the entity's clients and potential clients. You should take that perspective into account as you review the information the website makes available. If the report cites to primary authorities, that's helpful. And if the interests of your client correspond to those of the insurance provider, that perspective may help you understand your client's concerns. Citing the report would, in most circumstances, be inappropriate.

e. Articles in Forbes are addressed to an audience of business people. The article may alert you to some current (at least as of 2012) issues surrounding interlocking directors, but it is unlikely to do more than that. The article would do little to support a legal argument.

f. The good thing about this report is that it identifies the relevant statute in its title. While the report's focus seems to be on recent and proposed changes to legislation and regulations, it would almost certainly identify and cite relevant primary authorities. Its audience is presumably a group composed of current and future clients, probably a relatively sophisticated group. This report is probably a good source of information and a means to identify relevant primary authorities.

I.2. a. This is not a good way to start your research. At the beginning of your research you have no idea of what issues are raised, what authorities apply, whether this is a question of federal or state law, or whether a statute is likely to govern. When you know absolutely nothing about a topic, a reliable secondary source should be first on your research list. Reading a secondary source will help you determine how you will go about finding relevant primary authority, will highlight terms of art used in the subject area, and will summarize the most important issues. Moreover, entering the term "interlocking directors" in the search box of a commercial research database would not retrieve all the relevant cases. Some decisions may address the interlocking directors question by using other words (e.g., individuals who serve as directors on the boards of two companies that compete with each other) and a search for "interlocking directors" would not identify those cases.

b. Yes! Online versions of state and federal statutes in commercial databases such as Lexis, Bloomberg Law, and Westlaw include annotations to related primary and secondary authorities. That's a quick and easy way to identify important cases that interpret the statute.

c. It's not a good idea to start with the Restatements. We don't know if our fact-scenario involves issues of common law or is governed by statute. Restatements are most useful when the issue involves common law.

d. If you know nothing about a topic, you might look first to an introductory secondary source, rather than a treatise directed at the sophisticated practitioner. Once you know the lingo and understand the issues, turning to a practitioner-oriented treatise would serve you well. Although a practitioner-oriented treatise is likely to be very helpful to you later in your research, it's not the best place for a novice to start.

e. While some law review articles may help you identify the primary authority governing an area of law, there are better tools and sources for finding case law. Law reviews cite cases selectively, while resources such as ALRs are more comprehensive in identifying authorities from all jurisdictions across the country. Even the Restatements are likely to provide a more representative sampling of relevant case law than law review articles.

II. The question of whether an individual can recover for someone else's negligence when no physical injury was suffered is likely a question of state common law.

1. The Restatement of Torts may be an excellent source. If this is a question of first impression in your jurisdiction, you'll want to know how other jurisdictions address the question. If the issue is one that is well-settled in almost all jurisdictions, the Restatement will cover it. In addition to stating well-established common law, the Restatement includes citations to leading cases in the jurisdictions that follow the rule.

2. ALR articles summarize the law on a particular issue and provide citations to primary authorities. If you can find an ALR article on the topic, you will be a step ahead in your research.

3. Legal encyclopedias provide broad descriptions of legal doctrines and terms. While an encyclopedia may include an entry for negligent infliction of emotional distress, it will not analyze the issues nor will it provide more than a few citations to leading authorities. A legal encyclopedia is unlikely to be of much help in addressing your client's issue.

4. Unless you can find a law review article that surveys the treatment of negligent infliction of emotional distress in all U.S. jurisdictions, postpone turning to law review articles until you better understand the issues and have studied other jurisdictions' rules. A law review article that suggests or argues for a particular approach to the tort may be very useful as you develop your arguments. But it's probably not a good place to begin your research.

5. A treatise on torts, depending on its intended audience, may describe the elements of negligent infliction of emotional distress, analyze the doctrine as it has been adopted in different jurisdictions, provide examples of cases involving the tort, and suggest policy arguments related to the tort. While a treatise won't identify as many primary authorities as either an ALR article or the Restatement, it is likely to provide a more nuanced and thorough analysis of the doctrine.

6. Digests, the key number system in Westlaw, and the topic headnotes in Lexis are all tools that will help you identify cases that involve the tort of negligent infliction of emotional distress. These tools are often much more efficient in finding relevant case law than word searches (which can retrieve too many irrelevant results and which may exclude many relevant cases).

III. 1. The sentence purports to describe a federal regulation; it also references a definition set forth in a statute. There is no need — and it is inappropriate — to cite a secondary authority to merely restate a regulation or statute. Courts and professors alike will want to see citations to the regulation and the statute themselves, rather than a secondary authority.

2. There are a few things wrong with this paragraph. The first sentence is not supported by the quotation from Am. Jur. that follows it. And even if the quotation from Am. Jur. did support the claim made in the first sentence, Am. Jur. is not the kind of source that *best* supports the argument. The better authority to provide support for the first sentence is the California Law Review article cited later in the paragraph. But the sentence that follows — noting that Tennessee and North Dakota follow different rules — should be supported by citations to the Tennessee and North Dakota statutes themselves, rather than by a reference to a secondary source that may or may not describe those statutes. The last sentence of the paragraph cites, appropriately, a law review article — a good source to support a statement that commentators have argued for a change in the law.

3. This is exactly how the Restatements should be used. The writer cites a particular section of the Restatement to provide support for his statement that the law on a particular topic is well established.

Conclusion

Rose is a rose is a rose is a rose.
— *Gertrude Stein*

And, research is research. You are all skilled in finding information online, whether it's recipes and news or answers to questions and sports scores. There is no shortage of either information or tools to use to find it. The same is true in legal research whether on the open Internet or through commercial databases. Legal research is different only in that both the kinds of information you find — the authorities — and the way you use those authorities vary depending on the context and relationship among the authorities. We hope this book helped you to distinguish among and evaluate basic types of authorities, to balance their relative weight in different contexts, and to put those authorities to good use in your student writing and your practice. But, as is true for any book that you study in law school, this one is only an introduction. As you continue your studies and begin practice, your ability to research and write about the law will develop and improve. We hope you keep in mind some principles along the way.

WE'VE ONLY SCRATCHED THE SURFACE

I have always imagined that Paradise will be a kind of library.
— *Jorge Luis Borges*

This book focuses on the most fundamental of authorities — legislation, case law, and regulations — with a hint of secondary sources thrown in the mix.

A thorough understanding of those authorities will serve you well in law school, not only in your research and writing courses, but in your doctrinal and experiential classes as well. As you read cases, look at how judges write about authorities, and as you read statutes, think about the resources you would consult to interpret them.

As you have probably discovered for yourself, there are many types of authorities that we've not discussed; for every type of authority that we haven't described, there are appropriate and not-so-appropriate uses. The world is more and more interconnected, and our ability to access all kinds of information is ever expanding. Judicial decisions, documents filed with courts, and legal scholarship incorporate authorities from foreign jurisdictions and refer to other primary authorities like treaties, they find support for their arguments in data, and they rely on empirical studies and other disciplines' scholarship to provide guidance on policy and other questions. Legislatures consider the opinions of experts and their constituencies, they look to statistics, and they compare proposed legislation to the law in other countries. Agencies seek and consider input from scientists and other professionals, industry leaders, and the public. Even popular culture finds its way into the law.

The more you read — be that cases, appellate briefs, committee reports, law review articles, legal blogs, or anything else — the more you will see examples of how skilled jurists and practitioners use these non-traditional sources to accomplish a goal. You may also question how some not-so-skilled lawyers use those sources. Be judicious and thoughtful in considering how you might incorporate non-traditional resources in your research and writing. If you're making an argument, think about what other kinds of information — apart from primary authorities or legal scholarship — would support your claims. Evaluate the sources of that information much as you would evaluate traditional secondary sources. Does the author have particular expertise? Is the publisher reliable and will the source continue to be available when your reader looks for it? Is the information up-to-date? For what purposes was the information gathered or published?

We've not talked at all in this book about researching facts. A good part of your practice — whether you're a litigator or a transactional lawyer — will involve answering questions that really don't involve law. For example, you may need to find an expert for a products liability case, determine exactly when an event happened or when a deed was recorded, or figure out the opposing counsel's history in handling certain types of cases. As with primary and secondary authorities, this kind of information is often readily available; the harder part is figuring out what information would be helpful in different contexts and, again, evaluating the reliability and accuracy of the information you find. We hope that some of the principles for evaluating authority that we've emphasized in this book will be helpful in these other contexts as well.

PRACTICE, PRACTICE, PRACTICE

Great ideas originate in the muscles.
— *Thomas A. Edison*

To treat your facts with imagination is one thing,
to imagine your facts is another.
— *John Burroughs*

Understanding how to use authorities to accomplish a goal is not something that comes naturally. Law is different; its use of authority is unlike anything you encountered before you came to law school. Thinking like a lawyer means a few different things, but one thing it surely means is understanding the nature and use of authorities. The more efficient you are in identifying relevant authorities and the more practice you've had in applying those authorities to a problem, the better you will be at it.

Use the opportunities and resources available to you in law school to hone your research skills. Experiment using different resources — commercial databases, as well as publicly available online sources — and try different methods of searching for authorities and information within each one. You can arrive at a useful place in your research from many different starting points, and the best approach and starting point will depend on both what you hope to accomplish and your individual preferences. Those preferences will, of course, develop the more you research. To some extent, research is personal. Just as we all learn differently, so do we all research differently. Your comfort level in doing research will increase the more you do it; you'll develop confidence and mental models for approaching any research problem.

Research tools — the means by which we find authorities — will continue to improve as technology does; the methods you follow in your research process will improve as you gain experience and may change depending on the context of your research question. Your problem will not be finding sources, but figuring out which ones are most useful and then balancing and assessing them. And that's part of thinking like a lawyer.

Finally, don't forget print resources. Many resources (e.g., secondary sources that may or may not be law-focused) continue to be available only in print. For example, a book on the history of Jim Crow laws and their role in shaping elections and voting districts might be incredibly useful in redistricting litigation. Moreover, you may find yourself in a place that has print reporters and legislative codes, but no Internet connection. You should be flexible and knowledgeable enough to be able to find what you need absent a tether to the Internet. Finally, remember that the law was originally "published" in print. And the organization of those print publications made it easier for law students to distinguish among authorities and understand their differences. In an online world everything looks the same; we aren't able to see the khaki-colored bound reporters and distinguish those from the paperback volumes of the Code of Federal Regulations or the multi-colored federal and state statutory codes. Our legal citation system is based on print resources. Understanding the framework in which authorities are published in print will make those citation systems more comprehensible and easier to use.

RESEARCH: IT'S NOT A LAUNDRY LIST, IT'S A NETWORK

In every enterprise consider where you would come out.
— *Publius Syrus*

It's tempting to think of research as one stage in the process of solving a legal problem or determining how to counsel a client. And it is that; you begin most law tasks with research. But the process of solving a problem, writing a brief or a contract, or determining the consequences of a particular event is a recursive one. You may succeed in figuring out one aspect of your problem only to find that entirely new questions have come up, all of which require more research. In your first reading of a statute, you're unlikely to grasp all the elements, exceptions, and definitions; in your initial reading of a case, you're likely to miss the nuance. Research is not something you start, finish, and then move on to writing. You will need to keep researching as you write, counsel your client, and communicate with courts, agencies, and others.

Remember to adapt your research to your context and goals; think ahead about the governmental body and the kind of authority that is likely to answer your question. If a partner asks you to quickly find the elements of criminal assault, you would expect that question to be governed by state law and answered by a statute that sets forth the elements of the crime. If, on the other hand, she asks what needs to be proved to establish a tort claim for assault, you would expect state case law — ideally cases decided by the state's highest court — to provide the answer. Use your knowledge of doctrine to guide your research.

USE YOUR IMAGINATION[1]

What is now proved was once only imagined.
— *William Blake*

To invent, you need a good imagination and a pile of junk.
— *Thomas A. Edison*

The practice of law is rewarding because lawyers can help people solve problems, they can make the judicial system work more effectively, and they can contribute to the improvement of society as a whole. The practice of law engages and challenges us because it allows us to create solutions, improve our society, and seek justice. As lawyers, sometimes we piece together clues to solve puzzles, other times we build models to achieve goals, and still other times we hack through a jungle to find the light and the clearing deep within. In all of these efforts our success depends on our ability to understand the nature of authorities, to sometimes see them in new lights, and to relate them to other sources in possibly new and unexpected ways. Just as you perceive the color blue differently when it is next to green than when it is next to yellow, so does the usefulness of authorities change as we see them in new contexts. Every great leap and every small hop forward in law began with a study of the history that preceded it; the best lawyers are able to make unexpected connections and see undeveloped relationships among sources.

Far be it from us to equate authorities and junk. But Edison's need for a collection of raw materials corresponds to the lawyer's need for relevant sources. Inventors, artists, and attorneys can create something new and useful — and even something wonderful — when they apply an informed imagination to a collection of useful things. And those useful things — in law — can be found, understood, and used only with thoughtful research, careful reading, and an appreciation of how they fit into the universe of sources that make up the law.

We hope that you are inspired and challenged by your law school studies to do great things in the world and solve problems creatively. And we hope that this book helps you get started on that road.

---

1. For more on imagination and the law, see *The Legal Imagination: Studies in the Nature of Legal Thought and Expression*, by James Boyd White (Little, Brown and Company, 1973) and Carol Parker's article "A Liberal Education in Law: Engaging the Legal Imagination Through Research and Writing Beyond the Curriculum" in the first issue of the *Journal of the Association of Legal Writing Directors* (2002).

Finding Sources

The only thing that is constant is change.

— *Heraclitus*

Twenty years ago, lawyers and law students approached legal research as a treasure hunt — searching to find the elusive key that would unlock the answer to a legal question. Today, although some legal questions still require the diligent searching of a treasure hunt, much of the time legal researchers are instead learning to "sip from a fire hose" of information. Conducting research in the context of information overflow requires that students navigate the many sources available to them and understand how context affects the relationships among sources. Every chapter in the book helps you understand how to sort, choose, and use what you find.

Add to the hyper-availability of sources the fact that the details of how to use a particular finding method are constantly changing. Your authors decided that providing you with detailed screen shots of Google Scholar, Bloomberg, FastCase, Lexis, Loislaw, Ravel, or Westlaw on a given day would be a waste of your time. The details on the day we send this book to the printers might very well change by the time our first reader opens the book.

Still, even though nearly all students today understand how to use the Internet to find sources and are nimble when confronted with small changes in using a particular service, for those who would like a little help thinking about the finding process, this appendix is for you.

A NOTE ON PAPER SOURCES VS. ONLINE RESEARCH

Most of your research will be online. You can do the vast majority of what you need to do in legal research using online sources. Some information is only available electronically at a given moment. One thing to keep in mind, however, is that the designers of online resources often based their new resources on paper sources that legal researchers had been familiar with for many years. Thus, some online sources mimic the features of the original paper sources — features like an index, a table of contents, sidebars, or graphic representations of information. These features are just as helpful online as they are in books. Or perhaps you, like your authors, simply love the look and feel of working in books, so you may find occasion to do that. The principles in this book are true for online or paper sources.

ALGORITHMS

An algorithm is a formula or a set of rules that a computer follows in problem-solving calculations. Computers do only what they are told to do in code, step by step. The algorithm provides the steps to the computer. Those rules will determine both what the computer finds and the order in which the results appear to the reader.

A search engine may use many different algorithms, only some of which are available to the general public. For example, the most famous Google algorithm is PageRank, named after Google founder Larry Page. But Page-Rank is only one of many algorithms Google uses. Bloomberg, Lexis, and Westlaw most likely use different algorithms, which explains why you might do the same search in all three services and get different results.

Searches, regardless of the algorithm or method, present an important problem to researchers. If the algorithm or search formula you use is broad enough to find all relevant sources, the results will likely include more sources than the researcher can practically examine, including many that are mostly irrelevant. If it is so narrow that you get only directly relevant sources, you are probably missing something.

The trick is to balance these two problems. One way to do that is through the principles of weight of authority that we talk about in the book. You want to be sure that you find all the mandatory primary sources that govern your legal issue. Failing to find mandatory primary authority will be disastrous to your project. On the other hand, failing to find persuasive sources — especially when the issue you are researching is new or controversial — will short-change your client, because you will be unaware that compelling arguments can be made even in an area where the law appears at first glance to be well settled. Other ways to balance the two problems are to toggle back and forth between primary authority and secondary sources, to read the authorities carefully to determine which are the better reasoned, and to vary the kind of search you use between natural language searches and Boolean searches.

SEARCHES

Among the several types of searches a researcher might use, the most common involve either a "natural language" search or a "Boolean search with terms and connectors." A good researcher will know the difference as well as how to use each effectively. Further, an excellent researcher will quite often use both types of searches on the same project.

Natural language searches, sometimes called "descriptive term searching," are the default method of search in most of the search engines you'll use. For example, if you do a search in Google, Westlaw, or Lexis, you are doing a natural language search.

A natural language search uses a probability formula to determine the results according to the language of your search. This means that if probabilities indicate that two words in your search usually function in a certain relationship, the computer will search based on that probability. The order in which sources appear in the search results is also a function of probability. A natural language search puts more control in the hands of probability-based algorithms and less control in the hands of the researcher.

Natural language searches are often wonderful places to start because you most often find a few highly relevant documents. The problem is that they may not find all the results you need, nor do you have a way to control them. Additionally, natural language searches can sometimes be less helpful to novices who aren't familiar with the specific words, terms of art, or the relationships that will elicit the most useful results.

Boolean searches, sometimes called "terms and connectors searches," give researchers great control and flexibility. George Boole developed a system of logic that allows the researcher to input search terms that take into account relationships between sets of information. Here is a list of common Boolean connectors:

OR	expansive search for either of the terms	Ex: *attractive OR nuisance* will find all the sources that contain either the word "attractive" or the word "nuisance."
AND	more narrow search for all of the terms in the search	Ex: *attractive AND nuisance* will find all the sources that contain both words, but not necessarily the two words together. So you would get all the *nuisance* cases where the word *attractive* also appeared somewhere in the case.

BUT NOT	search that excludes a particular term	Ex: *nuisance BUT NOT attractive* would let you find *nuisance* cases that were not *attractive nuisance* cases
/number	search for numerical proximity	Ex: *attractive /1 nuisance* gets you results where "attractive" is used within one word of "nuisance." This search will find only cases where the court used the phrase "attractive nuisance" or "nuisance attractive"
/s or /p	search for proximity using grammar instead of numbers: /s is within the same sentence or /p is within the same paragraph.	Ex: *attractive /p nuisance* will find sources that have the words "attractive" and "nuisance" in the same paragraph, and could turn up *attractive nuisance* cases, but might also find results like this: "The plaintiff makes an attractive argument that the defendant was unaware of the condition. But a claim of nuisance does not require awareness of the problem."
Quotation marks	Search for what is within the marks exactly	Ex: *"attractive nuisance"* will only find sources that use the exact phrase "attractive nuisance."

Thus, if you want broad results, you use the "or" logic to get every source using any of the terms of your search. Alternatively, you use the "and" logic to narrow a search by requiring all of the terms you've connected with "and" to appear in your search result. Boolean searching also allows you to screen out certain results with the "not" logic. Other grammatical connectors also give you more control over your results. It is easy to find more elaborate charts of terms and connectors online.

Boolean searches will often help you find results you may have missed in a natural language search and vice versa. Google Scholar, Westlaw, and Lexis all have ways to refine your search from a natural language search to a "terms and connectors" Boolean search. Even with Boolean searches, however, the algorithm for different search engines may provide slightly different results. The database searched may vary as well. In addition to narrowing results with terms and connectors, other filters are available on all of the major search engines and may help you research more efficiently.

SORTING: FACTORS AS FILTERS

When we talk about choosing among sources in the chapters on weight of authority, cases, and statutes, we have emphasized both the context and the factors that influence the weight the current decision-maker is likely to give to the authority. Those factors include the specific relevance of the authority's content, as well as the factors that affect an authority's place in the hierarchy of authority: the jurisdiction, the type of authority, when the source came into being, its treatment and use by later authorities, and so on. These factors may be translated into "filters" on most of the major search engines. We will suggest some filters here, but you will be more successful if you first think about the weight of authority and the relationships among sources you will use to weave your arguments in a particular problem. Then you can use the factors derived from those principles as filters to narrow your search to the most relevant or useful sources.

The search engines in both public and commercial resources (like Google Scholar, Bloomberg, Lexis, and Westlaw) offer ways to filter or narrow your search results. Often you will find filters offered in a bar that runs down the left side of the page of your search. Here are some of the filters that may be useful:

Database content will naturally affect your search results. Choosing databases is the first step in conducting a search in the commercial services or in Google Scholar. The content of the databases on the commercial services may vary slightly, and checking the content is one way to be sure you've looked everywhere you want to search. Most often you will choose databases first according to whether the research involves an issue of federal or state law, then by selecting the appropriate federal or state jurisdiction. In many resources, you may narrow the database in which you search even more by using the hierarchy of authority within a particular jurisdiction: that is, you may search only for state Supreme Court cases within Arizona, or you may look first only at the Eighth Circuit Court of Appeals cases within the federal courts database.

Dates can make a difference in the weight accorded to the source. Additionally, sometimes more recent cases will helpfully summarize the development of the law on your issue in your jurisdiction.

Types of Sources are useful filters. You can start your research by looking at statutes rather than cases, for example, knowing that the statutory annotations will point you to relevant cases. Or you may start with cases, knowing that the cross-references to relevant statutes and to other cases will expand your research quickly. You may wish to get up to speed on the law with a useful summary in a secondary source. Or perhaps you wish to see proposed legislation. You can craft a search using these terms, or, in most services, you can apply filters to more general search results to help you find relevant sources.

Searching Within Results for Certain Terms or Relationships can often help you narrow a search that has provided too many sources to review efficiently. For example, if you narrow the search to a specific fact or facts found in your case, you may more quickly find the most analogous of the authorities, which may be the most helpful one to read first.

Citation Use and Treatment Using Citators or Other Services: As you read through cases interpreting the law, you will often see that one case or a handful of cases routinely appear in every opinion on your issue. You most likely want to cite to those favored sources. You can find them using updaters or citators like Shepard's or KeyCite. You can also use a service like Ravel.

UPDATING

Please remember your ethical obligation to check whether the sources you use are still good law. You can use Shepard's or KeyCite. Several other services are currently in the process of developing free or nearly free updaters.

PRINCIPLES TO KEEP IN MIND

1. *Begin with free methods whenever you can.* In practice you will need to keep costs under control, and commercial services are expensive. Develop strategies that minimize cost. Remember that once you understand better what you are looking for through your use of free sources, you can use commercial services efficiently to access only those things you need to buy.

2. *When choosing commercial services, look for added value.* Choose commercial services when either you can't find a free source for the information you want, or when a feature of the commercial service saves money when compared to the hours it would take to find the same result with free sources. For example, Ravel currently has a service that helps you quickly analyze which sources are groundbreaking, foundational, or landmarks within an area.

3. *As a student, your job is to gain enough experience working with various methods to be productive no matter what services your future employer may provide in the office.* Time is short for law students, but even shorter for lawyers. Now is the time to play! You'll need a preliminary familiarity with all of the most prevalent commercial services, and the best time to develop it is as a student, while the services are already part of your tuition. The paradox: you need to spend hours on the services to learn to spend only minutes on them.

4. *As long as you know your jurisdiction and have at least a general understanding of the legal question involved, it doesn't matter much which kind of source you start with — statutes, cases, regulations, or*

secondary sources. One kind of source will lead to another. Often your professor may suggest that you consistently use one step-by-step process or a certain kind of source first. Here are two examples of step-by-step processes professors typically recommend. There are others, and you will develop your own with practice. Remember, for class it makes sense to use the one your professor recommends.

a. 1. Start with a plan that takes into account the relative weight of authority and your initial impressions and expectations of what you are searching for.

2. If you are a novice or new to a particular area, begin by educating yourself and reading about your issue in secondary sources.

3. Use the secondary sources to find key primary authorities.

4. Expand and narrow the search: use specialized searches and filters to find your jurisdiction (primary mandatory authority) and then if necessary, move on to primary persuasive sources.

5. Update the sources you intend to use to be sure they are still good law.

b. 1. Find one good case or statute — however you want to find it.

2. Branch out using an updater like Shepard's or KeyCite both to check whether it's still good law, and to see newer sources citing your original source. The new sources are likely to address your issue.

3. Circle around: go to a secondary source or something you haven't looked at yet, just to check that you're on a good path and haven't missed anything.

As you gain experience, you will develop an instinct for what processes most often work well for you and how context may affect where you start. Remember that search algorithms have chosen the order in which sources appear. Nevertheless, *you* should be in charge of choosing among authorities that you determine are relevant to your issue.

5. *When you can't remember information about sources or the best principles about finding things, a simple general search will remind you.* Examples might be a Google search for "How do I make sure my case is still good law?" "What date did Alaska start putting legislative history online?" or "What is an ALR?"

6. *Government sources online are free and often overlooked by beginning researchers.* For example, FDsys (the "Federal Digital System," available at www.gpo.gov/fdsys) is the official federal government website for publications from all three branches of government. FDsys includes official online versions of the United States Code, the Code of Federal Regulations, and the Federal Register, among many other items. Other government sources provide other types of access to federal laws (e.g., federalregister.gov and regulations.gov), and the websites of many federal and state agencies provide reliable summaries and descriptions

of the legislation they implement. A list of some of these resources is at the end of this Appendix.

7. *Many nonprofit or public interest sites share a goal of making the law freely available.* Harvard University has just begun a project (Free the Law) to digitize its holdings of case law, and resources like CourtListener offer opinions and other documents, as well as oral arguments, from many jurisdictions. See the list at the end of this Appendix for more suggestions.

8. *Remember that lawyers often need information beyond sources of law.* Your research courses and this book focus on sources of law, but lawyers sometimes need to research information such as which party is likely to have the deepest pockets, the history of a company, or the public life of a party to the lawsuit. The best sources to find this information are beyond the scope of this text, but Google is a good place to start.

9. *Books!* Most commercial services do not include monographs or other books in their databases. Google Books for Academic Research is a place to start, but don't eschew the old-fashioned pleasure of browsing the relevant print collections in your law library.

UP-TO-THE-MINUTE HELP
AKA THANK GOODNESS FOR LIBRARIANS,
GOOD SAMARITANS, AND YES, THE GOVERNMENT!

Law libraries, especially those connected to law schools, provide expert guidance in how to do legal research. What's more, librarians are more conscientious than most about keeping guidance current. Most libraries offer free basic information, and many law school libraries offer video tutorials, charts, step-by-step guides, annotated lists of resources by topic, and clever or entertaining explanations that will help you learn and understand the research process.

The first library to check is your own school's. The guidance will be tailored to your library and will often include specialized information for your jurisdiction. Another value in starting with your own school's library is that you will also find a directory to librarians who may be available to help in person.

A Google search for "free legal research tutorials" pulls up many lessons, both written and video, from law school libraries. See the next page for a list of those we especially like.

Government sources can offer online instruction. For example, the Library of Congress has an excellent YouTube video on using Google

Scholar to find cases, and offers beginner's guides to everything from finding the center for presidential communications to lemon laws.

Other organizations can help too. The ABA (American Bar Association), CALI (Computer-Assisted Legal Instruction), and other non-profits also offer readily available instruction along with resources of primary and secondary authority.

Here are some lists of services or websites that have been relatively stable choices for the last five to ten years or more. We've arranged them by topic, but listed them alphabetically, and not in order of their utility. We offer no guarantee they will still be available by the time you read this, and the platform details may change, but these services have been widely available and many have found them useful:

THE MORE COMPREHENSIVE COMMERCIAL SERVICES (YOU NEED A PRELIMINARY FAMILIARITY WITH EACH OF THESE)

Bloomberg Law
Lexis
Westlaw

COMMERCIAL RESOURCES THAT ARE OFTEN FREELY AVAILABLE TO MEMBERS OF STATE BAR ASSOCIATIONS

Casemaker
Fastcase

OTHER ONLINE SERVICES

Bureau of National Affairs (BNA, often organized by topic)
HeinOnline (sources other than cases and statutes including law reviews, historical sources and much more)
Loislaw
Versuslaw

FREE OR NEARLY FREE SERVICES

Dragnet
The Public Library of Law (often included with state bar membership)
Justia
Google and related search engines
Google Scholar for case law
Google Books Academic
Ravel

GOVERNMENT AND OTHER NON-PROFIT SOURCES

congress.gov
Court websites (federal and state)
Agency websites (federal and state)
CourtListener

FDsys
Legal Information Institute
Library of Congress (Guide to Law Online)
Pacer (Public Access to Court Online Records)
regulations.gov
usa.gov
whitehouse.gov

SOME LAW SCHOOLS AND LAW SCHOOL LIBRARIES OFFERING ONLINE
RESEARCH GUIDES AND TOOLS

(These are some examples only! Many, if not most, academic law libraries
post research guides and tutorials on their websites, and many others
include current awareness resources that allow students and attorneys to
keep up to date on topics of popular interest.)

Cornell: Legal Information Institute
Georgetown Law Library: Research Guides
Harvard Law Library: Legal Treatises by Subject
NYU Law: Library Research Guides
University of Washington: Gallagher Library Research Guides
USC Gould: Law Library Research Guides
Washburn School of Law: WashLaw — Legal Research on the Web

Some Citation Basics

You need to let the little things that would ordinarily bore
you suddenly thrill you.
— Andy Warhol

WHY WE CITE

Citations function for our readers in important ways. A classical rhetorician
would say that citations are essential to persuasion. They bolster the writer's
ethos or credibility (showing the reader that the writer has done the
necessary research); they support the logos or logical force of an argument
(demonstrating whether there are controlling rules); and they strengthen
pathos, or the appeal to the reader's values (reinforcing a shared belief in
following the law).

Practically speaking, citations allow a reader to find the relevant authorities and then verify that the author has fulfilled the lawyer's duty of "Candor
Toward the Tribunal."[1] If your readers want to understand the context of the
decision you've cited, a correct citation means they can find it and read the
entire opinion. Another function is to fulfill the author's ethical duty of
attribution when using the ideas or words of another.

Furthermore, citing precedent is especially important in a justice system
based on a hierarchy of authority and the doctrine of stare decisis, which
requires deference to precedent. Arguments about the meaning or interpretation of statutory language are supported by citations to the text. We also
support arguments about controlling rules and analogous cases by citing

---

1. Model R. Prof. Conduct 3.3.

previous judicial decisions. With a citation, an argument becomes something greater than a clever lawyer arguing for a particular result, and instead is an argument supported by *the law* compelling a result. Readers need a shorthand that will tell them the weight of authority and thus the persuasiveness of each of the sources used to support an argument. You've learned that some authority is *mandatory or binding*. The citation shows the reader the year of a decision (or that a statute is currently in effect), the jurisdiction affected by the authority, and for cases, the level of the court issuing the decision and any important subsequent treatment affecting its worth as mandatory or persuasive authority. Readers will only be able to judge whether the strength of an authority demands attention when you provide a citation to show them.

MANY SETS OF RULES GOVERN CITATION: YOUR TASK IS TO LEARN TO USE ANY OF THE MANY CITATION RULES

Citation systems abound. And they change regularly as new editions of manuals are published, as courts change rules, and as new authorities and new formats for publishing authorities become available. Among the more famous citation systems are *The Bluebook: A Uniform System of Citation*; *The ALWD Guide to Legal Citation*; and the American Association of Law Libraries' *Universal Citation Guide*. A promising newcomer online is *The Indigo Book: An Open and Compatible Implementation of a Uniform System of Citation*, a free-content version of the 1958 edition of *The Bluebook*.[2]

The Bluebook: A Uniform System of Citation is recognized as the granddaddy of them all. It began as a style sheet for the law review editors of some prestigious law schools: Harvard, Columbia, Pennsylvania, and Yale. A style sheet is a list that authors keep of the choices they make as they write a document. For example, if an author decides on page 74 of a book to use the British spelling of gray — grey — then the author makes a note on the style sheet because she will want to do the same on page 121. Writing a style sheet is simply recording choices, and usually does not involve making up a logical system and then applying it. Thus, a style sheet may grow higgledy-piggledy. In the case of *The Bluebook*, the style sheet was written for scholarly articles in the law reviews. When courts began adopting *The Bluebook* as a part of their rules, the editors added a section of notes for practitioners. But the differences between rules written for scholarship and rules written for practitioners were complicated and at times confusing. And that's why *The Bluebook* has been awkward to use, and for years, it was every 1L's least favorite law book.

---

2. The authors of *The Indigo Book* chose the 1958 edition because the *Bluebook* editors had failed to renew that copyright.

Other guides were written in part because *The Bluebook* was so annoyingly complicated and frustrating to use. *The ALWD Guide* was adopted by many schools as a better teaching tool. *The AALL's Universal Citation Guide* takes into account that digital formats make page numbers obsolete. In response to competition over the years, *The Bluebook* and its competitors have all improved. But all of these guides may change a bit from year to year, so even if you've learned a system, you'll need to know how to check for changes. For the most important of primary authorities (i.e., cases, legislation, and administrative regulations), the rules of the several citation systems are very similar, if not identical.

Further complicating the citation landscape are "local rules." Remember that courts have the authority to make particular rules governing how each court operates. Citation rules are sometimes a part of the local rules. And the local rules can vary widely. For example, The *California Style Manual* states that an entire citation be cast as a parenthetical, which is not the norm in other places. Some New York courts expect the year of a decision to appear in between the parties' names and the volume number of the reporter when citing cases. Once you are practicing in a jurisdiction, it will be easy to find and adopt the local rules. Until then, you only need to understand that local rules vary.

Thus, it is really not a matter of which book or system you use in your first-year class in law school — instead, what matters is that you understand the purposes that citation systems serve, the general principles of how citation works, and how to find and follow the citation rules you need in a particular context.

PRINCIPLES TO KEEP IN MIND

1. *Citation choices involve "citation form" and "citation style."* Citation form means that you've written citations that conform to the rules of the system you're using. This often means being very careful about abbreviations, spaces between abbreviations, typeface, and exactly what to include in the citation. Worrying about citation form is like worrying about getting the right address on a very important letter; if it's not right, it won't be delivered or found.

   Citation style, on the other hand, is how you decide when to cite and where to place a citation. For citation form, you'll check the rules of the system your jurisdiction requires. For citation style, we recommend that beginners start by learning a few principles:

   A. *Include a citation after every sentence in which you make an assertion about the law*. This includes not only every time you state a rule in a sentence, but also every time you write a sentence about the provisions of a statute or regulation, the reasoning or the holding of a court opinion, or the facts of the precedent case. Sometimes that means that you will have a citation after nearly every sentence in the sections of documents where you explain or illustrate the law. Even if every sentence in a paragraph refers to the same source, the best practice is to cite after every sentence. If, on the other hand, the sentence is about how precedent applies in your new case, then you won't need to cite (as long as you have already cited the precedent).

B. *The modern trend is to avoid string citations unless the text supported by them makes claims about a number of courts or judicial decisions.* String citations — using more than one case to support the same assertion — don't make the support stronger. Use string citations only when the text makes a claim such as, "Four courts have found that. . . ." In that case you would need to cite cases in those four courts. But in general, showing that more than one judicial decision supports a proposition doesn't make it appear stronger.

C. *The modern trend is to place citations as a "citation sentence" at the end of a sentence of text, and not as a "citation clause" in the middle of a sentence.* Citation sentences follow a sentence of text. They end with a period. Here is a citation sentence:

> When a modification changes a game's essence, it alters an essential aspect of the game. *Kuketz v. Petronelli*, 443 Mass. 355, 364 (Mass. 2004).

Citation clauses come in the middle of a sentence and are set off with commas. Here is a citation clause:

> When a modification changes a game's essence, *Kuketz v. Petronelli*, 443 Mass. 355, 364 (Mass. 2004), it alters an essential aspect of the game.

2. *Good citation practice means that you can only assert what you have actually verified yourself.* When you cite, you are essentially saying to the reader: "If you look here, you'll find what I just paraphrased or quoted." You can do that only if you've looked there yourself. That means that if you read about a source in another source, good citation practice requires you to check to make sure the original source was correctly cited. For dates in citations to statutes or secondary authorities, it means you will cite the date on the source you viewed, not a previous or more recent version, unless you check that other version yourself.

3. *The first time you cite a source, use a full citation; if you cite the same source again within reasonable proximity to the first citation, you can use a short citation.* We'll look more carefully at short citations below, but

the guiding principle is reader comfort. Remember that one of our primary purposes in citing is for the reader to be able to identify, at a glance, the weight of authority and the nature of the source. Thus, you'll repeat full citations when there has been a significant lapse between the original citation and your new reference. But short citations are handy and interfere less, so use them when you can.

A BEGINNER'S GUIDE TO CREATING FULL CITATIONS TO STATUTES, CASES, AND REGULATIONS

You will need to learn to use a set of citation rules to cite more kinds of sources than we can introduce here. And you will need to feel comfortable using a manual for a system that is new to you. But we can give you a boost by setting out the most common citation forms for the sources you will use most often in court documents — statutes, cases, and regulations. This is the way most citation systems cite these sources.

There is an additional oddity that you should recognize about citation systems: although you likely will do most of your research in online sources, most guides to citation form are still based on print sources. For example, most cases are cited as they appear in reporters. A reporter — as we use the term now — is a set of books in which judicial decisions are published. When the notion of published case law was new, individuals served as "reporters," transcribing a court's decision, collecting all the decisions over a period of time, and then publishing those decisions in a series of books. Over time, the books themselves, rather than the people who reported the decisions, came to be known as "reporters." When we cite case law, we cite the decision as published — in print — in a reporter. You should visit your library and take a look at the print reporters in which court opinions are published, and you should leaf through the statutory codes in which federal and state statutes are collected. That way, you will better understand the references below, and in your citation manual, to the elements that go into the typical citation.

Remember that the citation rules — based, as they are, on print formats — are, in a way, vestiges of a bygone era, and consequently, may not seem to make much sense in a world where most primary authority is easily and freely available online. But their lack of trendiness, signs of age, and their insistence on citations for a stable medium like print ensure that the reader can identify the nature of the authority and its strength. Digital media can be ephemeral: websites come and go and URLs may change. Maintaining a system of citation to sources in print may ignore the realities of the modern day researcher, but it promises a reliable and stable identification of sources.

Basing citation on print sources results in another feature of citation you should understand, the parallel citation. Cases are often collected in more than one set of reporters: for example, U.S. Supreme Court cases can be found in the United States Reports, as well as in the Supreme Court Reporter. California state court cases can be found in the California Reports, West's California Reporter, and the Pacific Reporter, among others. Some of these are "official" reporters, and some are "regional" reporters (and some are both!). The various citation manuals and court rules have different requirements about which of the reporters should be cited in different situations. A good rule of thumb is to use the citation from the official reporter, if any exists. Citation manuals will indicate official reporters in the appendices that set forth abbreviations for primary sources in individual jurisdictions.

Let's take a look:

Statutes: Statutory citations vary widely by state, but most of the time, a full citation to a statute will include:

- the name of the provision, if the section you're citing has one
- the title number (if any)
- the abbreviation of the name of the code in which the statute is found
- the section symbol(s)
- the section number
- the date (this is usually the date of the publication of the statute in whatever resource you are citing, not the date of the statute's enactment or amendment)

An example: 42 U.S.C. § 12182 (2015).

42	is the number of the title within the statutory code.
U.S.C.	is the abbreviation for the name of the code, United States Code.
§	is the section symbol. If you can't make the symbol on your word processor, you can abbreviate it using "sec."
12182	is the number of the section you are referring to.
(2015).	is the date the statute you found was published.

Cases: A full citation to a case will tell the reader:

- the name of the case
- the volume numbers in each set of reporters in which it appears
- the abbreviation of the names of the reporters in which it appears
- the page numbers on which the case begins in each set of reporters

- the "pin cite," or the exact page number where your proposition appears in the original source
- a parenthetical that includes the date and identifies the court, if you cannot discern the court from the name of the reporter

An example: *Mapp v. Ohio*, 367 U.S. 643, 645 (1961).

Mapp v. Ohio	is the name of the case, consisting of the names of the parties that have been properly abbreviated as the rules of the citation system dictate. Also notice the name of the case is italicized, and there is a period after the "v."
367	is the volume number of the reporter series in which the case is reported or published.
U.S.	is the abbreviation of the "United States Reports," the name of the reporter in which you will find the opinion. Notice that we know from the name of the reporter which Court decided the case — here, the U.S. Supreme Court.
643	is the page number where the case starts in volume 367.
645	is the "pin cite," or the exact page number within the case where you will find the assertion you made.
(1961).	is the date the case was decided. Notice we already know the court because the reporter tells us which court decided the case (that reporter only includes cases from the U.S. Supreme Court). The parenthetical in the citation does not need to mention the court. And a period finishes the citation sentence.

Another example: *U.S. v. Weaver*, 808 F.3d 26, 28 (D.C. Cir. 2015).

U.S. v. Weaver	is the name of the case, consisting of the names of the parties properly abbreviated as the citation system directs. Also notice the name of the case is italicized, and there is a period after the "v."
808	is the volume number of the reporter series in which the case is published.
F.3d	is the abbreviation of the name of the reporter. Here, the reporter is the Federal Reporter, Third Series. The Federal Reporter contains cases from all federal circuit courts, and not cases from the U.S. Supreme Court or the federal district courts. But the name of the reporter doesn't tell us which of the circuits decided the case.
26	is the page number where the case starts in volume 808.

28	is the "pin cite," or the exact page number within the case where you will find the assertion you made.
(D.C. Cir. 2015).	Here the parenthetical includes both the court and the date. It includes the correct abbreviation for the court as established in the citation manual, because the Federal Reporter contains opinions from all of the federal circuit courts, and thus you can't tell from just reading the name of the reporter which court decided the case. Remember: for weight of authority purposes, you MUST be able to tell from looking at the full citation which court decided the case. A period finishes the citation sentence.

Let's look at differences in the citations of a state case as published in two different reporters. The first citation is to the official reporter.

State v. Summers, 182 Ohio App. 3d 139, 140 (2009).

State v. Summers	is the name of the case, consisting of the names of the parties properly abbreviated. Also notice the case name is italicized, and there is a period after the "v."
182	is the volume number of the reporter series in which the case is published.
Ohio App. 3d	is the name of the reporter. This reporter includes only cases from the Ohio intermediate appellate courts.
139	is the page number where the case starts in volume 182.
140	is the pin cite.
(2009).	is the date the case was decided. Notice that because the reporter tells us which court decided the case (that reporter only includes cases from the Ohio intermediate appellate courts), the parenthetical in the citation does not need to mention the court. And a period finishes the citation sentence.

Now look at the same case in a citation that locates it within a different reporter. But this time the reporter includes cases from many different state courts in a region.

State v. Summers, 935 N.E.2d 26, 27 (Ohio App. 2009).

State v. Summers	is the name of the case, consisting of the names of the parties properly abbreviated. Also notice the case name is italicized, and there is a period after the "v."
935	is the volume number of the reporter.

N.E.2d	is the name of the reporter. Here it is the reporter that includes cases from many courts regionally.
26	is the page number where the case starts in volume 935.
27	is the pin cite.
(Ohio App. 2009).	is the date the case was decided. Notice that because the reporter does not indicate which court decided the case, the parenthetical must include the proper abbreviation for the court. And a period finishes the citation sentence.

There's one more complication that comes up when researching and citing case law. As we mentioned in Chapter 4, some judicial opinions are "unpublished." Judges occasionally issue opinions that, by designation by the judge or the court, are not published in the official reporter. Those decisions usually have no precedential value under the court rules. But these purportedly unpublished decisions may, in fact, be published in unofficial reporters (like the Federal Appendix) and they are even more likely to appear in online resources. Citation manuals include formats for citations to unpublished opinions. The more challenging question for the researcher and writer, however, is whether those unpublished opinions *ought* to be cited in documents filed with a court. To answer that question, you will need to consult the court rules. Some courts prohibit citations to unpublished decisions, while others allow them.

Regulations: A full citation for federal regulations will include:

- the title number
- the abbreviation for the Code of Federal Regulations (C.F.R)
- the section symbol
- the section number
- the date

An example: 50 C.F.R. §100.26 (2014).

50	is the title number; here it's Title 50, Wildlife and Fisheries.
C.F.R.	is the proper abbreviation for the Code of Federal Regulations.
§	is the section symbol, or you can substitute "sec."
100.26	is the section.
(2014).	is the date of publication, and a period to end the citation sentence.

A state example: 112 Mass. Code Regs. § 1.20 (2016).

112	is the title number.
Mass. Code Regs.	is the proper abbreviation for the "Code of Massachusetts Regulations." You'll find the proper abbreviations and the way to cite individual state regulations in the appendices to either *The Bluebook* or *The ALWD Guide to Legal Citation*.
§	is the section symbol, or you can substitute "sec."
1.20	is the section.
(2016).	is the date of publication, and a period to end the citation sentence.

SHORT FORM

The rules governing the use of short citations depend on whether the citation follows directly after the full citation, or another citation intervenes between the original full citation and another reference to the source. The use of the short form may also depend on whether the textual sentence that the citation follows includes information about the source, such as its name.

Id.: "Id." is a short-form citation that you may use for statutes, cases, and regulations when you are citing the same source you cited immediately before. No other citations may intervene. When readers see Id., they look to the last citation before it to know your reference. If you are citing the exact same section or page, you may use a simple Id. If you are referring to the same source but to a different page or section, you should indicate that: Id. at 22 (22 is the pin cite.), or Id. at §203.

Other short forms:

Statutes: You will choose short citations for statutes that allow your reader to easily understand the statute or section to which you refer.

Full citation:	42 U.S.C. § 623 (1989).
Short citation options:	42 U.S.C. § 623
	§ 623

Cases: Again, you will choose short citations based on whether you are sure that your reader will easily recognize the case to which you refer. With cases, the short citation may take into account whether the case name appears in the textual sentence preceding the citation.

Full citation:	*Conneaut Lake Park v. Klingensmith,*
	66 A.2d 828, 831 (Pa. 1949).
Short citation options:	*Conneaut,* 66 A.2d at 831.
	66 A.2d at 831.

A few notes on the case citations and choices. First, the full citation above includes just the state name in the parentheses. This indicates the opinion was written by the Pennsylvania Supreme Court. The citation manual, in its appendices, sets forth the abbreviations for courts. Remember that if there were no intervening citation, you would use Id.

But when there has been an intervening citation, including the case name in the short citation is correct if the sentence the citation follows does not include the case name. The shortest citation above, 66 A.2d at 831, is correct when the sentence the citation follows indicates the case name. In our example, the sentence might read, "The Conneaut court stated that . . . ." Finally, note that you do not include the court and the date in parentheses in either short citation.

Regulations: Once again you will choose which short citation to use based on whether the reader will easily know the regulation to which you refer.

Full citation: 25 C.F.R.	§ 301.5 (2016).
Short citations:	25 C.F.R. § 301.5
	§ 301.5

A LIST OF THE MOST COMMON ERRORS BEGINNERS MAKE WHEN CITING THESE SOURCES

1. Failing to end the citation sentence with a period.
2. Failing to include the period after the "v." in case names.
3. Failing to include the date, or the court when necessary, in the parentheses.
4. Errors in abbreviations are common, especially in case names. Learn which tables in your citation guide set out the proper abbreviations. Tab your guide, so you can find them easily.
5. Failing to include the full case citation the first time the case name appears.

THERE IS SO MUCH MORE: LEARN TO USE A CITATION MANUAL

We hope we've given you a boost — an easy guide to the basic form for the most common kinds of citations you'll use in practice documents. But

Tip: For beginners, one way to learn citation format is to use the Westlaw or Lexis copy-paste option for the citation system you are following. After you locate an authority that you want to include in your document, you can easily highlight a few words and right click for the option to copy with a reference. Right click and both services currently let you choose which citation guide you want for the copy-paste. Paste the excerpt along with the citation into your draft. You will most likely delete the words you copied to get the citation unless you intend to quote, but you will have a basic citation you can correct, turning to and applying the rules in your citation manual. Like using a secondary source to understand an area of the law, the original citation format simply gets you started. After you have become accustomed to citation, you will no longer need to rely on this shortcut.

learning through trial and error to use a citation manual is important because you will need to understand many more citation rules. Citing constitutions, secondary sources, treaties, and emails are just a few examples of sources you might need to cite. Using typeface and spacing rules correctly is critical to creating a good impression by forming citations correctly. The signal rules (*See* or *See, e.g.*, for example) help your reader immediately understand why you've cited a case. And if you hope to represent your school as an editor on a law review or journal, you'll need to understand the citation rules for scholarly work. The reasons for learning to cite correctly are compelling. Perseverance and practice, not memorization, is the key.

Citation can seem like the most mundane and mechanical of tasks; ensuring correct citation formatting is a task loved by few and dreaded by most. But remember that your legal argument is only as strong as the authorities that support it; and, even if you have gathered substantial authority to support your position, no one will be able to appreciate your hard work, inventive analysis, and cogent arguments unless they understand and can refer to those supporting authorities. It's like stringing holiday lights on a house. You do all the hard work to lay out and connect the strings of lights; the last — and most essential — task is to plug the strings into the outlet. And that last detail is, as Andy Warhol suggests, where the thrill comes in.

Index